# Tales from the Viking Age

*Captivating Legendary and Historical Sagas*

© Copyright 2020
All Rights Reserved. No part of this book may be reproduced in any form without permission in writing from the author. Reviewers may quote brief passages in reviews.
    Disclaimer: No part of this publication may be reproduced or transmitted in any form or by any means, mechanical or electronic, including photocopying or recording, or by any information storage and retrieval system, or transmitted by email without permission in writing from the publisher.
    While all attempts have been made to verify the information provided in this publication, neither the author nor the publisher assumes any responsibility for errors, omissions or contrary interpretations of the subject matter herein.
    This book is for entertainment purposes only. The views expressed are those of the author alone, and should not be taken as expert instruction or commands. The reader is responsible for his or her own actions.
    Adherence to all applicable laws and regulations, including international, federal, state and local laws governing professional licensing, business practices, advertising and all other aspects of doing business in the US, Canada, UK or any other jurisdiction is the sole responsibility of the purchaser or reader.
    Neither the author nor the publisher assumes any responsibility or liability whatsoever on the behalf of the purchaser or reader of these materials. Any perceived slight of any individual or organization is purely unintentional.

# Free Bonus from Captivating History (Available for a Limited time)

Hi History Lovers!

Now you have a chance to join our exclusive history list so you can get your first history ebook for free as well as discounts and a potential to get more history books for free! Simply visit the link below to join.

Captivatinghistory.com/ebook

Also, make sure to follow us on Facebook, Twitter and Youtube by searching for Captivating History.

# Contents

FREE BONUS FROM CAPTIVATING HISTORY (AVAILABLE FOR A LIMITED TIME) ...... 1
INTRODUCTION ...... 3
THE SAGA OF KING HEIDREK THE WISE ...... 6
SELECTIONS FROM THE SAGA OF ÖRVAR-ODDR ...... 43
THE VOYAGES TO VINLAND ...... 62
REFERENCES ...... 91

# Introduction

Between the twelfth and the fifteenth centuries, Icelandic scribes were busily at work writing down what had formerly been orally transmitted stories containing both prose and snippets of poetry. Dubbed "sagas"—from the Icelandic *sögur*, meaning "story," "myth," or "history"—the manuscripts diligently copied by medieval scribes preserve histories and pseudo-histories along with imaginative works about dragons, giants, and larger-than-life heroes. Within the total corpus of Icelandic sagas are the *Fornaldursögur*, or "legendary sagas," and the *Íslendingasögur*, or "sagas of Icelanders," which are sometimes also known as "family sagas." These are two of the main subgenres of sagas.

As the name suggests, the legendary sagas are works of fiction. It is in these sagas that we meet all manner of fantastic creatures, read of the exploits of heroes and villains, and occasionally see the gods peek in to steer events or punish evildoers. The sagas of Icelanders, by contrast, are largely historical works that tell the stories of the families who left continental Scandinavian lands to settle Iceland beginning in the late ninth century. However, these historical sagas are not entirely untouched by the fantastic, since they also occasionally contain episodes that involve magic or the supernatural.

Before the advent of Christianity, writing other than runes used for inscriptions or incantations was unknown in Viking lands. Iceland was officially converted to Christianity around the turn of the eleventh century, so the stories that began to be written down in the centuries that followed occasionally are presented through a Christian filter, or have had certain aspects altered in order to conform with Christian doctrine and belief.

This current volume presents three Viking sagas. Two are legendary sagas, while the third is historical. *The Saga of King Heidrek the Wise* centers in part on the dwarf-made magic sword, Tyrfing. Tyrfing was originally made for King Svafrlami, but when he loses it in battle to Arngrim the Berserker, it becomes an heirloom of Arngrim's house, passed down from generation to generation. We can therefore see that even the legendary sagas can conform to certain features of the sagas of Icelanders through a focus on the story of a particular family, following the doings of each successive descendant, who functions as a protagonist in their part of the tale.

*The Saga of Örvar-Oddr* is a lengthy tale about the exploits of the hero Oddr. Doomed to live a 300-year lifespan only to be killed by a serpent hiding inside the skull of his long-dead horse, Oddr goes from battle to battle and raid to raid, conquering human opponents and giants alike. Oddr lives by both his wits and the strength of his arm which, as we shall see, comes in handy when dealing even with friendly giants. Oddr is something of a peripatetic hero, appearing in other sagas besides his own. We will have already seen Oddr fighting alongside his friend Hjalmar in *The Saga of King Heidrek the Wise* before we encounter him in his own tale.

The final saga in this volume is a historical one, dealing with the late tenth- and early eleventh-century Viking voyages to what is now northeastern Canada. The stories of these voyages are told in two historical works, *The Saga of the Greenlanders* and *The Saga of Eirik the Red*, which together are known as *The Vinland Sagas*. Here, we follow Bjarni Herjolfsson as he discovers this new land when he is blown off course on his way to Greenland, and then the voyages of Eirik's sons and daughter and others of Eirik's Greenland settlement, who make their own attempts to settle in a new place rich in wild grapes, salmon, and other good things.

Whether fantastical or historical, the Viking sagas show us very human characters behaving in very human ways. We see courage and villainy, sorrow and joy, and strength and weakness play out in these complex stories whose creators and first audiences lived over a thousand years ago.

# The Saga of King Heidrek the Wise

Like many other Icelandic sagas, The Saga of King Heidrek the Wise—which is also known as the Tyrfing Cycle and the Heverar Saga—is not solely about the title character but rather is a tale encompassing the history of several generations of the same family, of which Heidrek is but one descendant. In the first parts of the saga, we learn about Heidrek's forebears and about the history of the enchanted sword, Tyrfing. The earliest sections of the saga are relatively short, but each successive section increases in length until we get to the portion that deals with Heidrek himself, which forms the bulk of the narrative.

At first, it might seem difficult to understand how Heidrek merits the nickname "the Wise." Heidrek is malicious and impulsive, delighting in starting fights and sowing dissension among the men of his father's court. His final mischievous act at that court is to throw a stone that accidentally kills his brother, which leads to Heidrek's banishment. Before Heidrek is forced to leave, his father gives him some advice, which Heidrek vows to disregard. In the story that follows, we see how Heidrek's disregard for rules turns into a kind of wisdom all its own, although in the end, Heidrek must pay a heavy price for his ruthlessness and overweening pride.

Some readers may see echoes of this saga in the works of J. R. R. Tolkien. The magic sword Tyrfing seems to have been an inspiration for the elven swords that glow in the presence of orcs and that can slice through almost anything with ease, while Heidrek's riddle contest with Gestumblindi (literally "the blind guest") is reminiscent of Bilbo's exchange of riddles with Gollum in The Hobbit.

The version of Heidrek's saga presented here has been abridged to fit this book. Only a small number of the riddles in Heidrek's riddle contest with Gestumblindi have been included, and the part of the saga that tells what happened after Heidrek's death has been omitted except for a brief synopsis. The history of the kings of Sweden that ends the saga has been omitted entirely.

### Of Svafrlami

Once there was a king named Svafrlami. He was the son of King Sigrlami, who was the grandson of Odin. Svafrlami liked nothing better than to ride to the hunt with his friends. Often he could be found in the forest, his lance at the ready, and he rarely came home empty-handed.

One day, Svafrlami went out hunting, but as the day wore on, he became separated from his friends, and he found himself in a part of the forest he did not recognize. As the sun was setting, he came upon a large stone that stood in front of a cliff face. Two dwarves were standing outside the stone and clearly were making ready to enter the cleft behind it and so go to their homes. Svafrlami spurred his horse, and when he arrived at the stone, he jumped down quickly and put his sword between the dwarves and the stone.

The dwarves were afraid of this big, strong man who wielded a bright sword and rode a swift horse. "Please, do not kill us!" they begged. "We are just trying to go home! Let us go in peace!"

"First you must tell me your names," said Svafrlami.

"I am Dvalin," said one dwarf, "and this is my brother, Dulin."

"Ah, I have heard tell of you," said Svafrlami. "I have heard that you are the most cunning smiths in the world. I will let you go if you make me a sword the likes of which has never been seen. The blade must be so sharp that it can slice through the strongest steel as though it were parchment, and never will it have any speck of rust. The sword also shall make me invincible; I shall never lose a battle while I wield it, and never shall it miss a blow."

The dwarves reluctantly agreed to make the sword and set a day for the king to return to fetch it. Then the dwarves went into their mountain home, and Svafrlami rode away to find his way back to his own stronghold.

When the day came for the dwarves to give the sword to the king, Svafrlami arrived at the stone in the mountains to find Dvalin and Dulin standing outside, and in Dvalin's hands was the most beautiful sword Svafrlami had ever seen. It had a sheath and belt of the finest leather, and its golden hilt gleamed in the sun.

Dvalin gave the sword to the king and said, "Here is the sword you demanded. I give it to you as agreed, but to you I also say this: every time the sword is drawn, it must taste blood, and it must be sheathed again with that blood still upon it. Three crimes will be committed with this sword, and in the end, the sword will be the death of you yourself."

Svafrlami drew the sword and swung it at the dwarves, but they were too quick. Before the blow could land upon them, Dvalin and Dulin slipped into their mountain home, and the sword buried itself deep in the heavy stone that was their door. Svafrlami pulled the sword out of the stone, sheathed it, then mounted his horse and rode away, pleased with the dwarves' craftsmanship and scoffing at the curse they had laid upon him and upon the sword. The king named the sword Tyrfing, and whenever he carried it into battle, he was the victor.

Svafrlami married and became the father of a beautiful daughter named Eyfura. For a long time, Svafrlami's lands were peaceful and safe, for every time a foe assailed them, Svafrlami would challenge the other king to single combat. With the aid of the sword Tyrfing, Svafrlami conquered every enemy that dared take up his challenge.

This went on for many, many years, until Svafrlami was an old man. One day, a Viking named Arngrim left his stronghold on the island of Bolm and sailed to Svafrlami's lands, thinking to raid and pillage wherever he wished. When Svafrlami heard of Arngrim's arrival, he sent out a challenge to single combat, as was his wont. Arngrim accepted the challenge and met Svafrlami on the field of battle at the appointed time. The two warriors circled one another, holding up their shields and feinting with their swords while their armies stood at either side of the field, looking on. Soon the battle was joined in earnest, but it wasn't long until Svafrlami made one great sweep with his blade that sliced off the side of Arngrim's shield. Unfortunately for Svafrlami, the blow was aimed with such strength that the sword continued downward until its point became lodged in the earth. Arngrim seized upon this advantage by cutting off Svafrlami's hand at the wrist and taking Tyrfing for himself. Then Arngrim took Tyrfing and clove Svafrlami's body in two with it, and in this way part of the dwarves' curse came to pass, that Svafrlami himself would be killed by that enchanted blade.

With Svafrlami defeated, Arngrim and his warriors attacked Svafrlami's men, and soon Arngrim's army had the victory and went through the lands pillaging and taking captives, and there was none to stand against them. One of the captives was Svafrlami's daughter, Eyfura. Arngrim took her for his wife, and together they returned to his stronghold on Bolm.

### *Of the Sons of Arngrim*

Arngrim and Eyfura together had twelve sons. The eldest was named Angantyr, and after him followed in turn Hervarth, Hjörvarth, Saeming, Hrani, Brami, Barri, Reifnir, Tind, and Bui. There were also the twins, both named Hadding, who were the youngest children of the family. When all the boys had grown into men, Angantyr was the tallest and the strongest of all of them, while the twins were the smallest and the weakest.

But even the weakest of Arngrim's sons was stronger than most other men, and together the twelve brothers often took ship to go raiding in other lands. Never did they take anyone else with them, for no other help was needed, and they always came home with their ship heavily laden with booty. Soon they were so greatly feared that whenever their sail appeared on the horizon, the king of that place and his people would crowd onto the beach and there make a pile of their greatest treasures, so that the sons of Arngrim might take the gold and jewels and other goods and then leave without killing or taking captives or setting fire to roof and rick.

Now, each of Arngrim's sons had his own sword, and some of these swords became famous in story and song. Angantyr received Tyrfing as an heirloom from his father. Hervarth's sword was named Hrotti, and Saeming's was called Mistiltein. Tyrfing was the most powerful of all. It gleamed with a silver light when it was unsheathed, a light that came from the blade itself and that could even illuminate the darkness. Never could the wielder of Tyrfing return the sword to its sheath unless it had fresh blood upon the blade, and whoever the sword struck perished of the wound before the end of the next day, even if the wound was but very slight.

One Yule, the sons of Arngrim sat feasting and drinking, as was their custom. At the end of the feast, they passed around the pledge cup so that vows for the coming year might be made. When Hjörvarth received the cup, he said, "I vow that I shall go to Sweden and wed the daughter of King Yngvi. Ingeborg is the most beautiful maiden in the whole world, and only she is worthy to be my wife." Then Hjörvarth drank of the pledge cup, and so his vow was sealed.

The following spring, Hjörvarth and his brothers took ship for Uppsala. They went to King Yngvi's court, where they were well received. Yngvi granted them an audience in the chamber where he sat with his wisest advisers and bravest warriors, and at the king's side sat the lovely Ingeborg.

"Tell me who you are and what your errand is," said Yngvi, "and I will decide what is to be done about it."

Hjörvarth stood forth and said, "I am Hjörvarth, son of Arngrim. I have come to ask for the hand of your daughter, Ingeborg, in marriage."

"I see," said Yngvi, but before the king could say anything else, Hjalmar, Yngvi's bravest warrior, stood and said, "I ask you to let me speak, O King." The king nodded assent, so Hjalmar continued: "I have served you for a long time. I have fought to protect your people and your lands. I have taken wounds and shed blood on your behalf. I ask that you grant Ingeborg's hand to me, and not to this stranger whose life is spent in murder and theft."

Now Yngvi found himself in a quandary. If he gave his daughter to Hjörvarth, he would lose Hjalmar's loyalty and blood would be shed. If he gave his daughter to Hjalmar, Hjörvarth and his brothers would not leave until every last person in that chamber had been hacked to pieces and the stronghold looted and burned. Finally the king said, "You are both worthy suitors, but it is not my choice to make. Ingeborg must be the one to decide."

Ingeborg said, "If it is to be my choice, then I choose Hjalmar. I know him to be a good and honorable man. I would have a husband who knows what honor is, not some berserker whose hands are stained with the blood of so many."

Hjörvarth replied, "Very well, if that is your wish then so shall it be. But I challenge Hjalmar to meet me in single combat at midsummer. We will meet in Samsø. If you do not come, Hjalmar, I shall make sure that every man, woman, and child throughout every land knows that you are a rank coward and unfit to be wed to a highborn lady such as Ingeborg. You will not be able to show your face anywhere at all for shame."

"I am no coward," said Hjalmar. "I will meet you in Samsø at midsummer, and we shall see then who prevails."

Hjörvarth and his brothers sailed home and told their father all that had happened in Uppsala. "I like it not," said Arngrim when he had heard the tale. "Never yet have I had any cause to fear for any of my sons, but this to me bodes ill. Still, there is nothing to be done now; you must follow through with your challenge, Hjörvarth, or be named a coward yourself."

The sons of Arngrim stayed at their father's house throughout the winter. In the spring, they took ship for Samsø. On the way, they stopped at the stronghold of Earl Bjartmar, who had long been friends with Arngrim and his sons. Bjartmar caused a great feast to be held in honor of the twelve young men, and at the feast Angantyr asked for the hand of the earl's daughter, Svafa, in marriage. The earl and his daughter both consented, and so she and Angantyr were wed with great rejoicing.

Soon it was time for the sons of Arngrim to go to Samsø. Before boarding the ship, Angantyr asked to speak to his father-in-law. "My lord," said Angantyr, "I had a strange dream last night. I hear you are wise in these matters, so perhaps you might be able to tell me what it means."

"Tell me your dream, and I will do what I can," said the earl.

"I dreamed that we were on Samsø. There were a great many birds there, and my brothers and I slew them all. As we prepared to leave, two great eagles swooped down upon us. I fought with one eagle, and my brothers all fought against the other. But we were weak from having killed all the other birds, and so we all were overcome."

"There is no secret to this dream," said the earl. "It foretells the death of twelve fierce warriors."

Angantyr and his brothers then sailed for Samsø. When they arrived, they saw two ships in the harbor and rightly guessed that these were Hjalmar's ships. In fact, only one was Hjalmar's; the other belonged to Hjalmar's friend, Örvar-Oddr, who had come to Samsø to lend his support to Hjalmar if it was needed.

When the sons of Arngrim saw those ships, the berserker rage came over them. They boarded the ships, and although Hjalmar and Oddr's men fought bravely, they could not withstand Angantyr and his brothers. Soon every man aboard the ships had been slain, and the sons of Arngrim were roaring their way inland in search of Hjalmar.

Now, Hjalmar and Oddr had not been on the ships when the brothers arrived. They had gone ashore and walked inland, thinking to await Hjörvarth and thus be ready for the combat. Time passed, and when the challenger and his brothers had not arrived, Hjalmar and Oddr decided to walk back down to the shore to see whether anything had happened there. Not far from the beach, they came across the sons of Arngrim. The berserker rage had left them, making them weaker than they were at other times, and their swords were drenched in blood, telling the tale of their deeds upon the ships.

Hjalmar and Oddr paused. "Do you see what has befallen?" said Hjalmar. "They have already slain all our men and are likely to slay us as well. Doubtless we will be drinking ale with Odin in Valhalla tonight."

Oddr replied, "Valhalla may be a glorious place and Odin a gracious host, but I have other plans for tonight. We will kill each and every one of those berserkers, even though there are only two of us and twelve of them."

Heartened by Oddr's words, Hjalmar said, "So be it. We fight with those twelve, and we see who shall have the victory." Then Hjalmar said, "Look! Angantyr carries the sword Tyrfing. See how it shines? How shall we divide the fight? Will you take Angantyr alone and I the other eleven, or should I fight Angantyr and you his brothers?"

"I want to fight Angantyr," said Oddr. "Tyrfing is a mighty blade, to be sure, but my mail shirt is better than yours."

"Maybe so," said Hjalmar, "but I'm the leader here, and it's my honor that is at stake, not yours. I fight Angantyr, and you fight his brothers. I'll not have it said that I was afraid to face Tyrfing."

And so Hjalmar and Oddr went down to the beach and challenged Angantyr and his brothers. Hjalmar fought valiantly against Angantyr, and Oddr fought the other eleven, cutting them down one by one. When the battle was done, Angantyr and all the sons of Arngrim lay dead.

Oddr turned to Hjalmar, who was seated on the grass. "See?" said Oddr. "I knew we would be victorious! But why are you so pale? And your mail shirt is in tatters!"

Hjalmar replied, "I have taken sixteen wounds in my battle with Angantyr. You may not be Odin's guest tonight, but I surely will be. One of those wounds is just beneath my heart." Then Hjalmar took the ring from his finger and gave it to Oddr, saying, "Take this ring back to Ingeborg. Give it to her as a token of my love." Hjalmar took one last breath and then died.

Oddr made barrows for each of Arngrim's sons and laid them therein with all their weapons. Tyrfing was laid in the barrow with Angantyr. When this was done, Oddr took Hjalmar's body back to Sweden to be buried there, but once Ingeborg saw that Hjalmar was dead, she died of a broken heart, and the two were buried together in one grave.

### *Of Hervor, Who Also Bore the Name Hervarth*

In the court of Earl Bjartmar, Angantyr's wife Svafa was with child. When her time came, she gave birth to a baby girl, who she named Hervor. Svafa made her own father Hervor's foster-father, and both of them swore never to tell Hervor about Angantyr, lest she try to avenge him.

Hervor grew up tall and strong, and she had her father's berserker spirit. She was not content to stay at home and learn embroidery and other womanly arts; instead, she took up the bow and the sword and quickly became a more accomplished warrior and hunter than many of the fully grown men at the earl's court. When anyone tried to take away her weapons and set her to her needle, she ran away into the forest, where she lived like a highwayman, robbing any who came within sight. When the earl found out what Hervor had been doing, he sent men to the forest to capture her and bring her back to his court by force.

For a time, Hervor dwelt in her grandfather's house, but she was no more peaceful there than she had been in the forest. Often she amused herself by tormenting the slaves of the household. For a time, the slaves bore this ill-treatment without saying anything, but finally one of them could hold her peace no longer. "You are an evil person, Hervor, and you spend all your days doing evil things. But I suppose this is to be expected, given your parentage. Do you know why your grandfather has never mentioned your father's name? It's because he was nothing but a lowly swineherd, and you, in turn, have inherited that low nature."

Hervor then ran to her grandfather and demanded to be told the truth. "Was my father truly a swineherd? Am I truly the daughter of such a low-born churl?"

Bjartmar sighed. "No, Hervor, you are not the daughter of a swineherd. You are the daughter of Angantyr, son of Arngrim, and the blood of berserkers flows in your veins. Your father and his brothers were slain in battle on the island of Samsø before you were born."

When Hervor heard this, she dressed herself in men's clothing and found herself a sword and a bow with a quiver of arrows. She went to her mother and grandfather and said, "I can remain here no longer. I will take ship and live the life of a Viking. I will seek out the barrows of my father and my uncles. I will take Tyrfing for my own, and then I will avenge my father and all his brothers."

Hervor's mother and grandfather tried to change her mind, but Hervor would not be swayed. She changed her name to Hervarth and went down to the harbor, where she found a ship and a crew who were willing to go raiding with her. They sailed from place to place, looting as they went, but always Hervarth was thinking of her father and her uncles and what she must do to avenge them.

One night, Hervarth went to the captain of the ship and said, "We must sail to Samsø."

"I'll not sail there," said the captain. "That place has an ill name. It is haunted with all manner of spirits. If we go there, none of us will leave alive."

"We sail where I say we sail," said Hervarth. "And if you and the others are too cowardly to go ashore, you can wait for me in the ship. What I must do I must do alone, in any case."

"Very well," said the captain, "but if it goes ill for you with the spirits, we'll not come to fetch your body. You can rot there and be food for the ravens, if the spirits don't devour you first."

And so they sailed for Samsø, but when they arrived, the captain would not sail to the dock but rather anchored the ship in the harbor just as the sun was beginning to set. Hervarth took one of the small rowboats they had aboard and went ashore by herself. She began to walk inland, and soon came upon a shepherd gathering up his flock for the night.

"You there!" said Hervarth. "Can you tell me where the barrows of Hjörvarth and his brothers might be?"

"I can tell you," said the shepherd, "but if you have any sense, you'll stay far away from that place. And don't you see the sun is setting? It's not safe to be out after nightfall here. You should go back to wherever you came from."

"That I'll not," said Hervarth. "I fear neither man nor spirit. Now tell me, where are the barrows?"

"They are over there, beyond the forest," said the shepherd. "You'll know them by the flame that burns around them, night and day. Now, if you don't have the sense to go inside before it gets dark, I do."

Without another word, the shepherd called to his dogs and his sheep and set off for home.

Hervarth walked in the direction the shepherd had shown her, and soon enough she saw the light of the flames around the barrows. When Hervarth drew near, she saw that the fire was not something made and tended by human hands. Although the flames leapt high into the air, they did not consume anything around them, not even the dry grass at their feet.

Hervarth went through the wall of flames without fear and stood before the barrows of the twelve brothers. She looked upon the barrows for a moment, and then said:

*Wake, Angantyr!*
*Sfava's daughter*
*says to you, "Wake!"*
*Your only child, Hervor,*
*is here to wake you.*
*Wake, Angantyr!*
*Wake Saeming!*
*Wake Hjörvarth!*
*Give me the sword*
*with the bright edge*
*and the golden hilt,*
*the sword forged by Dvalin*
*for Svafrlami.*

When Hervarth was done with her incantation, the earth of one of the barrows stirred. A mist gathered on top of it, and from the mist arose the shade of Angantyr. The shade looked at Hervarth and said:

*Why wake me?*
*Why are you here?*
*Daughter mine,*
*this is no place for the living.*
*The blade you seek*
*is not here.*
*No kinsman buried me;*
*an enemy placed me here.*
*He placed me in my barrow,*
*the sword he bore away with him.*
*Seek it not!*
*It will be your doom.*

Then Hervarth said:

*I fear no doom,*
*nor the words of a shade.*
*Tell me no lies!*
*Give me the sword!*
*It is my birthright,*
*and it lies there*
*with you in your barrow.*

Angantyr replied:

*The sword shall you have*
*but not before*
*I speak to you your doom.*
*A son you shall have,*

*Heidrek will he be named.*
*Tyrfing will be his blade,*
*the strongest of men shall he be.*
*The blade is here,*
*beneath my back,*
*enwrapped in flame.*
*No woman has courage*
*enough to take it.*
Hervarth answered,
*Courage I have,*
*enough to take the sword.*
*I can see it now,*
*sheathed in flames.*
*If you will not yield it,*
*I will take it myself.*
*Even now*
*the flames subside*
*as I reach toward your barrow.*
Then the shade of Angantyr said,
*Very well!*
*Take it not;*
*I will give it you.*
*But it will bring only sorrow,*
*only grief, only ruin*
*to you and to yours.*
*Fare you well!*
*Would that I and my brothers*

*could rise and walk with you.*

*But that is not our fate.*

*Fare you well!*

When the shade of Angantyr finished speaking, it dissolved into mist. The mist dissolved back into the earth, and in its place atop the barrow was Tyrfing, with its sheath and belt. Hervarth took the sword and said:

*Fare you well!*

*May you rest here*

*undisturbed.*

*Go I must;*

*the barrow is no place*

*for a living woman.*

*Fare you well!*

Then Hervarth walked back through the wall of flames and set off through the forest. It had been a long journey to the barrows, and it was a long journey back. By the time she reached the shore, the sun was already peeking above the horizon, and in the dawn's light, Hervarth saw that her ship had already left the harbor, stranding her there on the island. She then went to the nearest village, where she was able to buy passage back to the mainland.

Hervarth traveled until she came to the court of King Gudmund. There she tarried for a time, but since she was still clad in men's raiment and still calling herself by a man's name, no one recognized that she was a woman. Gudmund and his courtiers were gracious to Hervarth, and treated her as though she were a man like themselves.

One day, Gudmund was playing chess and found that he was likely to lose. He sighed and then said, "I seem to be overmatched. Can no one here rescue me and turn the game to my favor?"

"I can do that, my lord," said Hervarth, and so Gudmund gave her his seat and she began to play. It did not take long for Hervarth to reverse the king's fortunes, but as she played, one of the courtiers took up her sword from the place she had laid it and turned it over in his hands, admiring the craftsmanship of the sheath and the hilt. Then the courtier drew the sword and said, "Here is a most noble blade, indeed! I have never seen one so fine!"

Now, Hervarth had been so engrossed in the game that she did not notice the courtier had Tyrfing in his hands until he drew it and began exclaiming. Straight away, Hervarth went to the courtier, wrested the sword from his grasp, and then struck off his head with the blade. She picked up the scabbard and belt, sheathed the sword, and left Gudmund's court.

All of Gudmund's warriors clamored to be allowed to follow Hervarth to have vengeance for killing their companion, but Gudmund would not allow it. "There is more to that Hervarth than meets the eye," he said, "and you will have small fame for his death, not least because I suspect that he is a woman. That woman is in possession of a mighty sword, and doubtless knows how to use it; I fear none of you would return alive from that quest. So this is my final word: no one will follow Hervarth. She leaves my court in peace."

For a time, Hervarth went raiding with the Vikings, but soon she became weary of that life. She took ship to her grandfather's court, where she was joyfully received by the earl and by her mother. Hervarth set aside her men's raiment and put on women's garb. She took her own name back and began to work at her embroidery. Soon the tale of the beautiful woman who had arrived at the earl's court made its way throughout the lands, and many young men thought to ask for her hand in marriage.

Now, King Gudmund had a son named Höfund, and he was a man both strong and wise. One day, Höfund went to his father and said, "Father, it is time that I took a wife. I come to you to ask your aid in this. Who would it be best for me to marry?"

King Gudmund said, "I know none who is more worthy than Hervor, granddaughter of Earl Bjartmar. It is she who should become your wife."

Höfund agreed to this, and soon King Gudmund sent emissaries to Bjartmar's court on that errand. Bjartmar received them well, and when Hervor learned that Höfund asked for her hand, she agreed to marry him. Soon all was prepared, and Höfund and Hervor were wed with great joy and feasting, and they lived together happily as man and wife.

## Of Heidrek

Höfund was the wisest of men, and all the people praised his good judgment. He was so wise that judges ever after were known as "höfund" in his honor. Whenever Höfund made a ruling, none dared go against it.

Höfund and Hervor had two sons. The elder was named Angantyr, and the younger was named Heidrek. Both of them grew into strong men, tall and fair of face. Angantyr took after his father. He was wise and wanted to do right by everyone. But Heidrek, whose foster-father was the hero Gizur, was the opposite. Heidrek was cunning and crafty, and he happily sowed dissension wherever he could.

There came a time when Höfund had a feast in his stronghold. He invited everyone to come and partake of the feast, except for Heidrek. When Heidrek found out about this, he was very angry and decided to go to the feast whether he had been invited or not. He also wanted to make mischief among his father's men in revenge for the slight.

Heidrek went to Höfund's stronghold and strode into the great hall as though he belonged there. Höfund and the other men glowered at Heidrek, not simply because he dared appear uninvited, but also because they knew no good would come of his presence there. Angantyr, however, rose and greeted his brother and gave him a seat beside him at the table. Heidrek took no joy in this, but rather sat there scowling.

After a time, Angantyr left the feast. Heidrek began to talk to the men who were seated on either side of him, lacing his talk with ill words that made one man think that the other was insulting him, while keeping himself out of the dispute. Soon the argument rose to such a pitch that it came to blows. Heidrek kept clear of the fighting, sitting back with silent pleasure at the malice he had wrought.

While the fight was still going on, Angantyr came back into the hall.

"What is this?" he said. "Why do you fight here in my father's hall, where all should be at peace with one another?"

The men stopped fighting and went back to their seats, but they were not at peace with one another.

After a little while, Angantyr left again, and Heidrek reminded the men about their argument. This caused the fight to resume, and it did not cease until Angantyr returned and told them both to make peace with one another. Again, Angantyr went out, and again Heidrek goaded the men into an argument. This time, one of the men took his knife and slew the other. Angantyr was very angry at what had happened, and when Höfund learned of it, he told Heidrek to go home and to stop making trouble.

Heidrek went out of the hall and Angantyr went with him, and they said their farewells to one another in the forecourt. Heidrek walked away, but he hadn't gone far when he decided there was yet more mischief to be made. He looked about on the ground and found a large stone. He listened and could hear people speaking to one another outside the hall. Heidrek hefted the stone in his hand, then threw it in the direction of the voices. From the sounds that followed, Heidrek knew that the stone had hit someone. He went to see who had been struck, and when he found that he had killed his brother, he ran away into the forest.

Heidrek regretted his deed, so in the morning he went back into the hall and told the whole tale to his father and mother. When

Höfund heard the story, he became very angry indeed. "This is a foul deed you have done, Heidrek, fouler than any other mischief you have accomplished so far. You have not only struck down a man from afar without giving him the chance to defend himself, but you have struck down your only brother. You deserve to hang for this, but I will not pass that sentence. Rather, you shall be an outlaw. Leave my realm, and never return, on pain of death."

Hervor was troubled by Höfund's judgment, for of her two sons she loved Heidrek best. "Surely, husband, this sentence is much too harsh? Should our son not be permitted to return to his parents at some time? Is he to lose all his inheritance?"

"My judgment stands, wife," said Höfund. "Heidrek is an outlaw from this point forth."

"If you will not relent," said Hervor, "then at least give him some good advice before he departs."

"He does not deserve anything, not even good words," said Höfund, "but because you ask, I will give."

Höfund turned to Heidrek and said, "Here is my advice, although I doubt very much that you will follow it. First, never help a man who has betrayed his lord. Second, never protect a murderer. Third, do not let your wife go home to visit her relatives, no matter how she might beg for this. Fourth, do not dally overlate with your mistress. Fifth, when you are in a hurry, do not ride your best horse. Sixth, do not be a foster-father to the child of a man who is of a higher status than yourself. That is all my advice, though likely you reckon it of little value."

Heidrek said, "I hold your advice in low regard because it was given with ill will. I am not obliged to follow even one word of it." Then Heidrek turned on his heel and left the hall, and in a moment his mother followed him.

"Heidrek, my son," said Hervor, "you have truly done yourself ill this time. Höfund will never relent, and you will never be able to return. But I will give you some gifts before you depart. Here is a purse full of gold, and here is a sword. This sword is Tyrfing, and it once belonged to my father, Angantyr the berserker. It is a famous blade; everyone has heard of it. It is also a victorious blade; whenever you draw it, you will be victorious. Now you must go. Farewell." Then Hervor went back into the hall, and Heidrek walked away to find his fortune as an outlaw.

After Heidrek had been journeying for some time, he came across a group of men. One of the men was bound with ropes.

"What has this man done that you bind him so?" asked Heidrek.

"He betrayed his lord," said one of the men of the group.

"Will you accept ransom for him?" said Heidrek. "I'll give you half of the gold in my purse if you let him go."

The men conferred among themselves and then said they agreed to Heidrek's terms. Heidrek gave them the gold, and then they lost the other from his bonds.

"Thank you for sparing me," said the man who had been bound. "In return for your kindness, I offer you my service."

"That service I'll not accept," said Heidrek. "A man who is willing to betray his own lord is likely to do the same to me. Go your own way; I never want to see you again."

Heidrek resumed his journey, and soon he came upon another group of men leading another man who was bound with ropes, as the first had been.

"What has this man done that you bind him so?" asked Heidrek.

"He is a murderer," said one of the men of the group.

"Will you accept ransom for him?" said Heidrek. "I'll give you half of the gold in my purse if you let him go."

The men conferred among themselves and then said they agreed to Heidrek's terms. Heidrek gave them the gold, and then they lost the other from his bonds.

"Thank you for sparing me," said the man who had been bound. "In return for your kindness, I offer you my service."

"That service I'll not accept," said Heidrek. "Someone who is willing to murder one man is likely to do the same to me. Go your own way; I never want to see you again."

Heidrek wandered the world for a long time until he finally came to Reidgotaland, where a man named Harald was king, who made Heidrek very welcome. Harald was now of a great age, and he sorrowed that he had no heir to take the throne after him. But that was not the end of Harald's troubles. Some of his earls had risen up against him, and in order to prevent war and the loss of his throne, Harald had agreed to pay them heavy tribute.

One day, Heidrek saw a great pile of treasure being heaped up in the forecourt of Harald's stronghold. Heidrek went to Harald and said, "What is this? Is this tribute that you are receiving from lands you have conquered?"

"Would that it were so!" said Harald. "But alas, no. This is tribute I must pay to my earls."

"Surely this is a shameful thing for a king such as yourself!" said Heidrek. "Why do you not resist?"

"Because this is the price of peace. I am too old to fight them any longer, and I do not wish them to wreak havoc among my people if I fail to pay. Besides, when I have faced them in the past, it has gone ill with me and my men."

"My lord, let me lead your army against these earls," said Heidrek. "I owe you a debt of gratitude for your hospitality, and it pains me to see a king of so great a kingdom reduced to paying tribute to his own earls."

"Very well," said the king. "You may lead my army against them, and if you defeat these earls, your reward will be great indeed. But I rather fear that it will go ill with you, and that you will not return to my house when all has been done."

Harald then placed his army under Heidrek's command, and all was made ready to assail the lands of the rebellious earls. Heidrek led the army into the territory of one earl after another, pillaging and slaying as they went. When the earls heard what Heidrek's army was doing, they summoned their own host and went out to meet him. Soon the two armies met, and battle was joined. Heidrek rode at the head of his army wielding Tyrfing. Every man that Heidrek faced he slew, for Tyrfing went through helm and shield and mail like a scythe through hay. Heidrek fought his way through the press of men until he found the earls, and then slew every last one of them. When the earls' men saw that their leaders had been killed and that the better part of their army already lay dead on the field, they fled, and the day was Heidrek's.

When the battle was done, Heidrek went throughout the earls' domains and told the people that they now owed tribute to Harald. He collected the tribute and returned in triumph to Harald's stronghold.

"Welcome, indeed!" said Harald when he saw Heidrek's return and the huge amount of treasure he brought with him. "You have saved my kingdom and enriched it besides. Anything you ask for, I will give you."

"I ask the hand of your daughter, Helga, in marriage," said Heidrek, "and for half your kingdom."

"They are both yours, with my blessing and with my great thanks," said the king.

### *Of Heidrek's Kingship*

Heidrek and Helga lived together very happily. They had one son, whom they named Angantyr, and Harald in his old age finally had a son of his own, who was named Halfdan.

For a time, all went well in Reidgotaland. Heidrek and Harald ruled wisely and well, and the people prospered. But then a great famine came, a famine such as no one could remember having come before. King Harald and Heidrek went to the soothsayers to ask what might be done because their people were starving, and nothing they had tried did any good.

The soothsayers cast lots and read the augury. They told the kings that the only way to appease the gods was to sacrifice the most noble boy in the land.

"Surely your son is the most noble," said Harald. "He should be the one sacrificed."

"No, it is your son who is nobler than mine," said Heidrek. "Halfdan should be the sacrifice."

The two kings argued about this for a long time. Finally, they decided to submit their quarrel to King Höfund, since he was the only one wise enough to judge the case. Heidrek was made leader of the embassy, which included the chiefest nobles and wisest counselors of both his realm and of Harald's. When the embassy arrived at his father's court, they were made very welcome.

Höfund heard the case and then pronounced judgment. He said, "Heidrek's son, Angantyr, is the noblest in the land. It is he who should be sacrificed."

"Very well," said Heidrek, "but if my son is the one to die, what should I get as recompense?"

"You should demand that every other man of the embassy who accompanied you here should be given over to your service," said Höfund. "After that, it will be up to you to decide what is to be done next."

Heidrek and the others went back to Reidgotaland. Heidrek told Harald what the judgment had been, and Harald agreed. He handed over the men to Heidrek, and a time and place were fixed for the sacrifice. But instead of preparing for the ceremony, Heidrek mustered his army and marched on Harald. There was a great battle, and at the end, Heidrek fought and killed Harald. Then Heidrek claimed that all of Harald's realm was now his, and that the sacrifice to

Odin was to be the dead who now lay slain on the field. When Helga learned what her husband had done, she was so distraught over the death of her father that she hanged herself.

There came a time when Heidrek summoned his army and went campaigning with them in the south. They went to the land of the Huns, where the king was named Humli. Heidrek defeated Humli and took Humli's daughter, Sifka, captive. For a time, Sifka lived with Heidrek as his mistress, but when she was got with child, Heidrek sent her back to her father. Sifka gave birth to a boy who was given the name Hlöd. Hlöd was raised by his grandfather, Humli, and was said to be the most beautiful child ever to be born.

Another time, Heidrek mustered his army and went to Saxland, thinking to conquer it. When the king of Saxland saw Heidrek's army, he sent an embassy to sue for peace. Heidrek accepted, on condition that the king give his lands to Heidrek and his daughter in marriage besides, for she was a very fair maiden, and Heidrek had heard tell of her great beauty. The king of Saxland agreed, and so there was a great feast held to celebrate the peace and the wedding of Heidrek and the king of Saxland's daughter. Heidrek greatly increased his wealth and his realm on this errand, and had become a very great king thereby.

From time to time, Heidrek's wife would ask leave to go to Saxland to visit her father. Heidrek of course granted her permission since he had yet to go against that piece of Höfund's advice. On these occasions, the queen would often take little Angantyr with her.

One summer, Heidrek had gone out raiding with some of his men. Their journey brought them close to Saxland, so Heidrek decided to row ashore in a little boat, accompanied by one other. They went at night, silently beaching their boat and then creeping toward the king's stronghold. Heidrek and his companion went to the window of the chamber where Heidrek's wife was wont to sleep, and they peered inside. There they saw the queen, asleep in the arms of another man who had long, golden hair. Little Angantyr was in a cot of his own in another part of the room.

"Surely you will slay them both?" said Heidrek's companion. "No king should have to live with that shame."

"No, I'll not slay them," said Heidrek.

"You've killed other men for far less."

"Yes, but I wish to do something else this time."

Heidrek evaded the watchmen and crept silently into the bedchamber. He took his knife and cut a great lock of hair from the man's head without waking either him or the queen. Then Heidrek picked up the sleeping Angantyr and bore him away back to his ships.

In the morning, Heidrek sailed into the harbor and was greeted with great rejoicing. The king of Saxland called for a feast, and when Heidrek was seated in the hall, he said, "I see my lady queen, but where is my son?"

A silence fell.

The queen said, "I have sad news to impart. Angantyr died in the night. That is why he is not here."

"Dead? My son? I don't believe it," said Heidrek. "Show me his body."

The queen brought Heidrek to the place where she said Angantyr's body was. Heidrek undid the wrappings around the corpse and saw that the creature inside was a dog.

"Well!" said Heidrek. "My son truly is in a sorry state, if he is not only dead but also turned into a dog!"

Then Heidrek sent for Angantyr, and when the boy entered the hall, Heidrek produced the lock of hair from his purse and said, "Here you see my son, quite alive, and not a dog at all. Now I would like to know from which of you I took this lock of hair."

Heidrek had the lock of hair matched to every man at the court, but it belonged to none of them. Then Heidrek began looking among the servants and slaves of the place until he came to the kitchen, where one of the slaves had a cloth wrapped around his head.

Heidrek tore the cloth off the man's head and held up the lock of hair.

"Surely none will say that this is not his hair," said Heidrek, and everyone had to admit that it did belong to the man.

Heidrek went to the king of Saxland and said, "You have always been a gracious host and have always been at peace with my realm. I'll not make war on you because of this, even though I have just cause. But your daughter I return to you; I want her no longer."

Then Heidrek left that court with Angantyr and sailed back to his own kingdom.

The next summer, Heidrek decided it was time for him to go against another of his father's counsels. Heidrek summoned messengers and sent them to the king of the Gardar in Gardariki to ask to be allowed to foster the king's son. The king of the Gardar heard Heidrek's request and said to the messengers, "I have no mind to send my son to King Heidrek. He is an evil man, cunning and crafty, and I do not wish my son to live with him."

But the queen said, "Think what you are saying, my lord! King Heidrek may have an evil reputation, but he is also a very mighty king, and everyone knows how ruthless he is. If you refuse this request, he may become angry. It will go ill for us then."

And so the king of the Gardar relented and sent his son to be fostered by Heidrek. The young boy was made very welcome in Heidrek's court. Heidrek was a good foster-father to the boy, teaching him all the things he needed to know and loving him as though the boy were his own.

At that time, Sifka, the daughter of Humli, the king of the Huns, had returned to live with Heidrek. Heidrek's counselors did not trust Sifka, and so they told the king not to let her know anything that would better be kept secret. Heidrek said that he understood their concerns and would keep their counsel in mind.

The son of the king of the Gardar had been at Heidrek's court for a few years when a messenger came to invite Heidrek to a feast in Gardariki. Heidrek of course accepted with many thanks. He went to Gardariki, bringing with him the king's son and Sifka. When they arrived, the king of the Gardar made them very welcome, and a great feast was held.

The feast went on for many days, and on one of those days, the men of the court took their hounds and hawks and went out hunting. During the hunt, the men separated into different parties. Some went this way, others went that, and Heidrek and his foster-son soon found themselves alone near a solitary farmstead. Heidrek said to his foster-son, "I have a task for you. Go to that farmstead, and hide yourself well. Stay there until I send for you." Heidrek then removed a ring from his finger and gave it to the boy. "Take this ring as payment. Now go."

The boy hesitated. "I do not think this is proper for me to do," he said, "but since you ask it, I will go."

Heidrek watched until he saw the boy slip into the barn unobserved. Then he returned to the king's court, where he assumed a sorrowful expression and refused company.

Sifka saw Heidrek's demeanor and wondered what was wrong. "Has something happened, my lord?" she said. "Why so sad when all others here are rejoicing?"

"I must not tell you," said Heidrek, "for if word got out, surely the king would have my head struck from my body."

"Come, now," said Sifka, "tell me what is wrong. You know I love you and that I would never betray you."

Heidrek continued to refuse her request while Sifka caressed and kissed him, thinking to persuade him to confess his secret in that way. Finally, Heidrek gave in and said, "I will tell you, but you must not say a word to anyone else. Do you so swear?"

"I so swear," said Sifka. "Now tell me what troubles you."

"My foster-son and I went hunting with the king's men. We found ourselves alone in an apple orchard. The day had been long, and the boy was hungry. He asked me to get him an apple from one of the trees, since he was not tall enough to reach one himself. Without thinking, I drew my sword and cut down an apple for him, but when I went to sheathe the sword, I found I could not do it. Then I remembered Tyrfing's enchantment, that it cannot be sheathed once drawn unless it has tasted blood. So, I cut off the boy's head with the sword and hid the body. That is why I am uneasy, because once the king finds out, he surely will have me killed."

The next day, the king of the Gardar held a drinking party in the great hall. Everyone sat along the tables and drank as much ale as they liked. Sifka was seated next to the queen of the Gardar. The queen turned to Sifka and said, "Your Heidrek certainly is gloomy these days. He's hardly touched his ale at all. What is the matter? Is he ill?"

"Oh, no, my lady," said Sifka, "he is not ill at all. He is sad because he slew your son and is afraid of what will become of him."

Sifka told the queen all that she had learned from Heidrek, and when her tale was done, the queen got up from the table and rushed from the hall, shedding many sorrowful tears. The king saw his queen leave, so he went to Sifka and said, "I saw you holding converse with my lady queen. What did you say to her to distress her so?"

"If it pleases my lord," said Sifka, "I only told her what chanced between King Heidrek and your son at the hunt yesterday. Heidrek has slain the boy; when the queen heard the news, it grieved her, and so she fled the hall, weeping."

The king of the Gardar became very angry. He called for his men to seize Heidrek. "Take that man prisoner!" he commanded. "Throw him in shackles that he might answer for his crimes!"

The king's men sat in silent puzzlement. They all liked Heidrek very much and could see no reason why he should be put into chains. Then two men stood forth and said, "We will do this thing, my lord," and they seized Heidrek, bound him, and made him stand before the king of the Gardar. These two men were the ones that Heidrek had ransomed from their bonds many years ago.

Heidrek, meanwhile, sent one of his men to fetch the young prince while the king of the Gardar summoned his court to hear the charges against Heidrek. The king told the people what Sifka had told him, that Heidrek had killed his son. Then the king said, "For this foul deed, Heidrek, I command that you hang by the neck until dead, like the murderous dog that you are."

Just as the king pronounced his sentence, the young boy came running into the court. "Father!" he cried. "Please don't kill him! I am alive and well, and King Heidrek has done nothing to harm me. He has been the best of foster-fathers, and you have no reason to hurt him at all."

Heidrek was released from his bonds and immediately made ready to depart. The queen of the Gardar saw that Heidrek was still very angry about what had happened, so she went to the king and said, "It is shameful to allow Heidrek to depart without some recompense. Offer him something in redress, and be reconciled to him."

The king agreed that the queen's advice was good, so he went to Heidrek and said, "I would that we might be friends again. I wish to give recompense for the shame you suffered at my hands. I have a great store of gold and would willingly part with every coin of it to redress your hurt."

"I have gold enough," said Heidrek. "Keep your treasure."

The king went away sad that he could not appease Heidrek. When he told the queen what had passed, the queen said, "If he will not take gold, then offer him your best liegemen and a share of your realm. Surely he will not be able to refuse such a gift."

The king went to Heidrek and said, "If you will not take my gold, then take my best liegemen to be your own and as large a share of my realm as you care to have. I give all to you very willingly to mend the hurt I have caused."

Heidrek said, "I have men enough, and my dominion is already very large. I will not take any of that from you."

Again, the king went away sad that Heidrek would not take what was offered. He told the queen what had happened, and she said, "If he will take neither gold, nor men, nor lands, then give him your most precious possession. Offer him your daughter's hand."

"I had hoped that would not be necessary, but I now see the wisdom in that. I shall do as you suggest."

The king went to Heidrek and said, "If you will take neither treasure, nor men, nor lands, then perhaps you will consent to wed my daughter? I have nothing more precious, and it pains me that we should part without reconciling."

Heidrek accepted this gift and so made peace with the king of the Gardar.

When Heidrek returned home, he decided that he needed to be rid of Sifka. He summoned her and said, "Make ready to leave. We go on a journey together."

Sifka did as she was told. She met Heidrek in the courtyard, where Heidrek's best horse stood saddled. Heidrek put Sifka on this animal, then took the reins and led it away from his stronghold. They walked for a very long way, until the horse finally became so exhausted that it fell down and would not rise. Heidrek left the horse where it was and commanded Sifka to walk. They went on until they came to a river that was both wide and deep. Sifka said, "How am I to cross such a river? I have not the strength to do this."

Heidrek said, "Climb up on my shoulders, and I will carry you across."

Sifka did so, but in the middle of the stream, Heidrek tossed her off his shoulders. He grabbed her body and broke her spine, then dumped her into the river, where she floated away with the current, dead. Then Heidrek returned home and commanded a great wedding feast to be held. He married the daughter of the king of the Gardar. Together they had a daughter named Hervor. She was fostered in England by Earl Frodmar and became a shieldmaiden, and she was as doughty as the strongest warrior.

## Of Heidrek and the Riddle-Contest

Heidrek had now become a very wealthy lord and the king of a wide realm. All the lords of the lands around respected him, and many paid him tribute. Having finished his days of conquest, Heidrek set about putting order in his kingdom. He declared that all disputes would be heard by a group of twelve judges chosen from among the wisest men of the land, and that their word should decide the cases brought before them. Heidrek also bred a special boar that he dedicated to the god Frey. The boar was nearly as large as a full-grown ox, and its coat was made of the softest, finest hair that shone in the sun like gold.

Now, it became the custom for all the men of Heidrek's court to gather at a feast on the eve of Yuletide, and at this feast, they would make their vows for the coming year. But instead of drinking the pledge cup, they would place one hand on the golden boar's head and another on his back and so make their vows, swearing by the great animal beneath their hands. One Yuletide Eve, the men took their turns swearing their oaths on the great boar, and when Heidrek's turn came, he said, "This I swear by Frey's golden boar: that whosoever shall go before the twelve judges and have his case go against him, that man will receive his freedom if he comes before me and bests me in a contest of riddles."

It came to pass that a man named Gestumblindi fell afoul of Heidrek, who summoned him to answer before the twelve judges. Gestumblindi knew that the judgment was likely to go against him, so he offered many sacrifices to Odin, praying that he might be delivered from his fate. On the evening before the trial, Gestumblindi sat staring into the fire, worrying about what might chance in the morning. He sighed and stood up from his chair, thinking that he might as well go and sleep. When he turned away from the fire, he saw a man standing before him. The man was dressed in rough traveler's clothes and a wide-brimmed hat. He had a mighty spear in one hand and a patch over one eye. This was none other than Odin himself, who had heard Gestumblindi's prayer.

"Peace, Gestumblindi," Odin said. "Be not afraid, for I have received your sacrifices and have come to help you. This is what you shall do: On the morrow you shall not go to the trial. You shall remain here at home. Hide yourself, and let no one see you, for I shall take your shape and go in your stead, and all will be well." Then Odin vanished, leaving a trembling and grateful Gestumblindi standing in an empty hall.

In the morning, Odin took on Gestumblindi's shape and went to the trial. The judges heard the evidence and decided against Gestumblindi. "You have heard the judgment," said the king. "Will you take your punishment, or will you face me in a contest of riddles?"

"I know you to be a crafty and cunning man," said Gestumblindi. "I fear that whatever I do, the end will be the same for me."

"Be that as it may," said the king, "you still must decide here and now which path you will take."

"Very well," said Gestumblindi. "I will play at riddles with you."

"Good," said the king. "Ask me a riddle, and if I cannot answer it, you will go free. If I answer all your riddles, the punishment stands."

"Here is my first riddle," said Gestumblindi.

*I left my house and went on a journey.*

*I journeyed over a road made of roads.*

*There was a road above me*

*And a road beneath me*

*And roads on every side of me.*

*What is the answer to my riddle?*

"Ah, that is an easy one," said the king. "You crossed a bridge, and there were birds flying above you and to the side of you. The bridge went over a river that had fish swimming in it. Tell me another."

Gestumblindi said,

*Yesterday when I awoke, I drank a drink*

*that was not wine, nor was it ale,*

*and I neither drank mead nor ate food,*

*yet I slaked my thirst.*

*What is the answer to my riddle?*

"This is a good one," said the king, "but I know the answer. You lay on the grass, and when you woke, you lapped up the dew that had fallen. Tell me another."

Gestumblindi said,

*Who is it that shrieks?*

*as he walks on hard paths*

*that he treads over and over?*

*Two mouths he has*

*and is always kissing,*

*and the path he treads is made of gold.*

"This one is obvious," said Heidrek. "It is the hammer used by a goldsmith, and its shrieks are the sounds made when it strikes the anvil. Have you no better riddles?"

Gestumblindi said,

*I pass over the ground*

*swallowing forest and field as I go;*

*I flee before no man*

*but I run when the wind blows,*

*and always I battle with the sun.*

"That is fog," said Heidrek. "It enwraps and enshrouds everything and blots out the sun, but the wind can blow it away. Do you have another riddle?"

Gestumblindi said,

*Maidens are we,*

*running all together*

*as our father chases us.*

*Our hair is pale*

*and our hoods are white,*

*and no man shall ever know us.*

"I know this one," said Heidrek. "Those are waves. Tell me another."

Gestumblindi said,

*Four I have that dangle down,*

*Four I have that tread the ground.*

*To show the way out I have two*

*and also, to keep away dogs.*

*A filthy one dangles behind me.*

"Ha!" cried Heidrek. "That is easy. It is a cow. Have you no better riddles?"

Gestumblindi said,

*I am two that runs*

*with ten feet and three eyes*

*and I have but one tail.*

"That is Odin when he rides upon Sleipnir," said Heidrek. "Make your next riddle more difficult."

"This riddle will be my last, and you will know the answer only if you are truly the wisest of all kings," said Gestumblindi. "Here is my riddle: What did Odin whisper in Baldur's ear before kindling his pyre?"

"Who else but you would know the answer?" cried Heidrek as he drew his sword and slashed at Odin. But Odin turned himself into a hawk and flew away, and the blow only severed the end of his tail feathers. This is why hawks have short tails today.

Then Odin took his own form and said, "Heidrek, you have tried to kill me without just cause, and for this I pronounce your doom: You will die a lowly death, slain not in battle by a warrior but murdered in your bed by a slave." Then Odin vanished, leaving Heidrek to ponder what he had said.

Now, some years ago, Heidrek had gone raiding and had captured nine slaves. These slaves were all noblemen, and they chafed at being held in thrall. They were always looking for ways to escape and bided their time patiently until they saw their chance.

That chance came when one-night King Heidrek went to his chamber to sleep. He had few guards, and the night was moonless and still. The slaves found themselves weapons and crept into the king's hall and then down the corridor to where the king slept. They killed the guards and went into Heidrek's chamber, where they slew him in his bed. Thus, perished King Heidrek the Wise.

In the morning, Angantyr, the king's son, called a great council where he announced the death of King Heidrek. The nobles one and all declared that Angantyr should be the king of the realm, and Angantyr accepted. "However," he said, "the murderers of my father still run free. I shall not assume the throne until I have found them and have avenged my father."

Angantyr had a reason to find the slaves other than vengeance, for when the slaves slew the king, they also took Tyrfing from his bedside and carried it away with them. Angantyr was not lightly to be deprived of his birthright, and so he went in search of the slaves meaning to kill them all and take Tyrfing back.

One evening, Angantyr found himself walking along the mouth of the river Grafa, where he saw three men in a boat, fishing. As Angantyr watched, one of the men caught a fish on his line and landed it in the boat.

"Pass me the bait knife, will you?" said the man who had caught the fish.

"You'll have to wait," said the other. "I'm using it right now."

Instead of waiting, the first man took a sword from the bottom of the boat. He drew the sword and used it to cut off the fish's head. Then the man said,

*A pike it is who loses its head*

*in payment for Heidrek's death*

*here at Grafa-mouth*

*at the feet of the Harvathi Mountains.*

When Angantyr heard this, he knew that the men were three of the escaped slaves and that the sword was Tyrfing. Angantyr watched as the fishermen finished their work and then rowed back to shore. He waited in the forest until night fell, and then sought out the place where the slaves had made their camp. He crept into their camp as they slept, then pulled their tent down upon them and slew them all. Then he took Tyrfing and went back to his stronghold, having avenged the death of his father.

*The next episode of the saga tells of the conflict between Angantyr and his half-brother, Hlöd. Hlöd goes to Reidgotaland to demand his share of the inheritance. Angantyr makes a generous offer, although it is short of an equal division of Heidrek's lands and treasure. Gizur, Hlöd's foster-father and one of Angantyr's courtiers, thinks that less than a half share is still too great, considering that Hlöd's mother was a war captive and bondmaid. Hlöd is greatly insulted by this. He* returns home and tells his grandfather, Humli, the king of the Huns, that Angantyr refused to share the inheritance equally. Humli assembles a great army to challenge Angantyr in revenge for the insult. The battle goes on for eight days. On the last day, Angantyr kills both Hlöd and Humli, much to his sorrow, and the Gothic warriors rout the Hunnish army.

The final portion of the saga is a concise history of the kings of Sweden from Angantyr's grandson, Ivar the Wide-Grasping (r. c. 655–c. 695), to Filip Halstensson (r. 1105–1118).

# Selections from The Saga of Örvar-Oddr

We have already met the hero Örvar-Oddr in King Heidrek's saga, where he accompanies his friend and blood brother Hjalmar to a battle to determine whether Hjalmar is fit to wed the daughter of King Yngvi In addition to guest appearances in other sagas, Oddr is also the subject of a saga of his own, which tells of his birth and childhood, his travels to far-flung places such as Ireland and Permia (an area around the Kama River in what is now Russia), his battles with Vikings and giants, and of how he marries and becomes a king.

Örvar-Oddr's name literally translated is "Arrow's Point." (Other versions of the name in modern sources are Arrow-Odd and Orvar-Odds.) His given name is Oddr ("Point"), but the rest of the moniker was added by a giant who saw some magic arrows that Oddr had in his quiver and dubbed him "Örvar-Oddr." Unlike many ancient heroes, Oddr has two human parents and a relatively normal birth, but when he grows up, he has a hero's strength and skill and has his family's uncanny ability to get the wind to rise merely by hoisting a sail. Oddr also is headstrong and irreverent, a trickster at one moment and a fearsome warrior the next.

As is proper for such a hero, Oddr is the subject of a prophecy about the manner of his death: A venomous serpent hiding inside the skull of a horse named Faxi will bite him. Oddr takes measures to defeat the prophecy, but no man can defy fate. When Oddr returns to Berurjod, where he was fostered, he prods the skull of a horse that he finds lying on the beach, and as predicted, a venomous serpent strikes from underneath, and Oddr dies from the serpent's venom.

Oddr's saga is too long to present in its entirety in this book, and so only a select few episodes are retold here.

### The Childhood of Örvar-Oddr

Once there was a man named Grim Hairy-Cheeks who lived in Hrafnista in Norway. Grim was the son of Ketil Trout, and he was a very wealthy and very well-respected man. Grim's wife was Lofthaena, the daughter of Harald, chieftain of Oslofjord. Lofthaena was very beautiful and quite the cleverest woman in all of Norway. Grim loved her very dearly and couldn't bear to deny her whatever she wished.

One day, Grim decided to sail to Oslofjord to attend to some business he had there. He intended to go without his wife on this particular journey because she was heavily pregnant with their first child, and he did not want anything to endanger her. But when Lofthaena heard he was leaving for Oslofjord, she demanded to go along. Grim tried to dissuade her, but Lofthaena insisted, and so Grim allowed her to come with him.

Grim fitted out two fine ships, and on the day, they were to depart, they had a fair wind. They had sailed as far as Berurjod when Lofthaena cried out. "Husband," she said, "we must put ashore right away. My pains are upon me."

Grim immediately ordered his ship to sail for land. They put ashore near the homestead of a man named Ingjald, who lived there with his wife and their young son, who was named Asmund. Grim sent messengers to Ingjald's house to ask for help, and when Ingjald heard the message, he hitched his horses to a cart and went to the beach himself to see what might be done for Lofthaena and Grim.

"Please come up to my home," Ingjald said. "We are well prepared for guests, and my wife and the other women of my household will be more than happy to help yours with her labor."

Grim and Lofthaena gratefully accepted Ingjald's invitation. They rode up to the house in his cart, and there Lofthaena was given into the care of Ingjald's wife, while Grim was shown to the high seat in Ingjald's hall to await the birth of his child. Ingjald was the most gracious of hosts; his guests lacked for nothing and were treated with great honor.

Lofthaena came through her delivery safely. Her child was a lusty boy, and all the women of the household said they had never seen a more beautiful baby. Lofthaena held her son and said, "Take him to his father so that he can get his name."

The women took the baby to Grim, who was delighted to see his new son. Grim named him Oddr and sprinkled him with water.

After three days in Ingjald's house, Lofthaena said that she was ready to resume the journey to Oslofjord. Grim went to Ingjald to let him know that they were leaving.

"Before you go," said Ingjald, "won't you honor me with a gift?"

"Most assuredly I will," said Grim. "My wife and I are in your debt for your hospitality, and I am very wealthy. How much of my money would you like to have? Whatever you ask, it will be yours."

"I don't want money," said Ingjald. "I have plenty of my own."

"That's fine," said Grim. "Ask me for something else, then."

"Give me your son to foster," said Ingjald.

"I am willing, but first I need to ask the boy's mother what she thinks," said Grim.

When Grim asked Lofthaena about allowing Ingjald to foster Oddr, Lofthaena said, "Our host honors us with that request. Let Oddr stay here as Ingjald's foster-son."

Ingjald saw his guests down to their ship for their departure. Little Oddr stayed behind at the house with Ingjald's wife. There was a fair wind, so Grim and Lofthaena sailed quickly and safely to Oslofjord, where they conducted their business. When this was completed, they sailed for home.

As they approached Berurjod, Grim said to Lofthaena, "Shall we go to Ingjald's house so that you can visit your son?"

Lofthaena answered, "There is no need. I saw him before we left, and I don't think he was sorry to see us go. Let's continue on our way home."

And so Grim and Lofthaena went back to Hrafnista, while Oddr stayed at Ingjald's house and was brought up with Ingjald's son. Ingjald raised Grim and Lofthaena's son well. He even thought more highly of Oddr than he did of his own son.

Oddr was the strongest and best-looking of any of the boys for miles around. He learned to play sports and to shoot with a bow and arrow, although he was a very serious boy and didn't play games like children usually do. As soon as Asmund and Oddr were old enough, they became blood brothers, and Asmund was with Oddr wherever he went.

Oddr was very fond of archery. He collected arrows from every arrow maker he could find, but he did not keep the arrows properly. He left them lying about everywhere so that people were forever tripping over them in the dark, or worse, sitting on their points by accident. This happened so often that people began to complain to Ingjald.

"You really must do something about that Oddr and his arrows," they said. "The situation has become quite annoying, and besides, it's dangerous."

Ingjald agreed to speak to his foster-son about this. He went to Oddr and said, "If you're not careful, you're going to have a very bad reputation very soon."

"Why is that?" said Oddr.

"You leave your arrows strewn about everywhere. People have been tripping over them and even sitting on them, and they're so tired of this that they've begun to complain about it."

"That's no fault of mine," said Oddr. "You've never made a quiver for me to put them in."

"I'd be happy to give you a fine quiver," said Ingjald. "Just tell me what you want."

"Oh, I don't think you'll be happy about this at all," said Oddr.

"I gave you my word," said Ingjald. "Ask."

"Take the black three-year-old goat that's in your herd. Kill it and skin it, but leave the horns and the hooves attached. Make me a quiver out of that hide, and mind you keep the horns and hooves as part of the quiver."

Ingjald saw to it that the quiver was made exactly as Oddr had requested. Oddr put all his arrows into it. It was a large quiver, bigger than anyone else had, and full of arrows that were longer and stronger than the arrows anyone else used. When the quiver was full, Oddr had himself a bow made to match the arrows.

Oddr liked to dress well. He had a fine red tunic that he liked to wear every day, and a gold headband that he put around his head. Everywhere he went, he took his quiver and bow with him. Oddr had one other peculiarity: He did not believe in the gods and refused to offer any sacrifices. "I'm strong enough to look after myself," he would say when people asked him about this. "I don't need a god's help to do what needs doing."

Asmund joined Oddr in this refusal, and in this they were both unlike their foster-father, who regularly offered sacrifices to Odin and the other gods. Asmund also joined Oddr in his boat, and the two of them often could be seen rowing up and down the coast together.

## The Prophecy

Once there was a wise old woman named Heid. She had the gift of sight and would travel around the country telling people what their fates would be. One day, she went to visit one of Ingjald's neighbors, and Ingjald heard that she was a guest there.

Ingjald went to Asmund and Oddr and said, "I have something I need you to do for me."

"What is that?" said Oddr.

"The seeress Heid is visiting not far from here," said Ingjald. "I've prepared a feast for her. I want you to invite her here so that she can tell everyone their fates."

"Absolutely not," said Oddr. "I don't want that old witch anywhere near me. Don't you dare have her in this household."

"Very well," said Ingjald. "Asmund can do the errand alone just as well as in your company, and he's more obedient, anyway."

"Don't send Asmund by himself either," said Oddr. "If that witch comes here, I'll have to do something to show you how very displeased I am."

In the end, Asmund went by himself to invite Heid to be a guest in his father's house. Heid gladly accepted and came to Ingjald's homestead with the fifteen boys and fifteen girls that attended her everywhere she went. When Heid arrived, Ingjald came to meet her at the door with all of the men of his household. Ingjald invited Heid inside and made sure she had everything she needed for the fortune-telling, which was to be on the day after the feast. Heid and her followers feasted well with Ingjald and his household, and when the meal was done, Ingjald and his people went to bed while Heid and her followers left the house to do the rituals needed for the fortune-telling.

In the morning, Ingjald went to Heid and said, "Did your rituals go well? Are you ready to tell us our fates?"

"They went well," said Heid. "I am ready."

Ingjald gathered his household together. "Sit down, everyone. We'll go up one at a time for Heid to tell us what is in store for our futures."

As the head of the household, Ingjald went first. He stood before the old seeress, who said, "I am glad to see you here, Ingjald. Your fate is to be respected and honored by everyone for the rest of your life."

Ingjald was very pleased with this. He thanked Heid and went back to his seat.

Asmund took his turn next.

"I am glad to see you here, Asmund. You'll have a good reputation far and wide. You'll not live to a great age, but everyone will know how brave you are, and what a fine warrior."

Asmund thanked the seeress and went back to his seat. Each person in the household took their turn hearing their fate from her, and no one left disappointed. After Heid had spoken with everyone in turn, she made some prophecies about the winter to come and about many other things. Ingjald thanked her well when she was done.

"Now," said Heid, "are we sure that I've seen everyone in your household? I don't want to leave the job unfinished."

"I think so," said Ingjald.

"What's that over there on that bench?" asked Heid.

Ingjald glanced in that direction. "Oh, that's just a cloak that someone left behind."

"It's an odd cloak that twitches whenever I look at it," said Heid.

No sooner had Heid said this than the person under the cloak sat up. It was Oddr, who was furious that Ingjald had invited the seeress there against his wishes.

"Yes, this cloak twitches, because I'm right here underneath it," said Oddr. "And I'll tell you what I want from you: I want you to shut up and go away. You're not wanted here. There's nothing you can tell me about my future, so you need to leave right now."

Oddr was holding a stick, which he showed to Heid. "See this stick? I'll whack you with it if you breathe one word of prophecy about me."

"I'll not be silent," said Heid. "It's my duty to tell the fate of everyone who comes before me. Besides, you'd do very well to listen to me." Then Heid spoke this prophecy:

*You fail to frighten me*
*Oddr, Ingjald's foster-son.*
*Your stick is not stronger*
*than my seeing,*
*and always I speak true.*
*Run and roam as you might,*
*on wave, on shore,*
*fate always finds a man*
*no matter where he goes.*
*Bound you shall be*
*by your destiny*
*to die here at Berurjod.*
*From the skull of Faxi*
*the sly serpent will strike.*
*Venomous fangs*
*will find your heel,*
*dealing out death to you*
*after you have lived a long life.*

Then the seeress said, "I have this also to tell you: Your life will be many times that of other men. Three hundred years will you wander the world, and everywhere you go you will conquer. But it won't matter how well you fight or how well everyone esteems you; the skull of the horse Faxi will be your doom, right here in Berurjod. There is no way you can escape your fate."

"Shut up, witch!" cried Oddr. "I told you not to say anything at all about me!"

Then Oddr hit the seeress in the face with his stick, breaking her nose and covering her face with blood.

"I'll not stay here a moment longer," said the seeress. "Get my belongings. I'm leaving. Never have I ever been treated this way in a place where I made prophecies."

"Please don't leave," said Ingjald. "Allow me to recompense you. I have many valuable gifts to give you if you stay here for three more nights."

"The gifts I'll take in redress for my injury," said the seeress, "but I'll not stay a moment longer."

As soon as Ingjald had given the old woman the gifts he had promised, she left his house and never came back.

When the seeress had gone, Oddr went to Asmund and said, "Come with me. We have a job to do."

Oddr and Asmund went to the stables, where they found the horse named Faxi. They bridled the horse and then led it away from the house and into the woods. They found the place that Oddr was seeking, and there they tied the horse up while the two of them dug a deep pit. By the time they were done digging, the lip of the pit was many feet above their heads. Once Oddr was satisfied that the pit was deep enough, they killed Faxi and pushed his body into the pit. Then Oddr and Asmund gathered many large stones and pushed them into the pit on top of the horse's body. Over each layer of stones, they poured a layer of sand to seal up the cracks between the stones, and they did not stop until they had raised a large mound over the horse's grave.

When the work was done, Oddr looked at the mound of stones and smirked. "Let's see whether Faxi's skull can manage to get out of that," he said. "That'll teach that old witch to make prophecies about me. There's no way anything she said is going to come true."

Oddr and Asmund returned to the house, where they went to speak to Ingjald. Oddr said to Ingjald, "Give me some ships."

"What for?" said Ingjald. "What are you planning to do with them?"

"I'm leaving," said Oddr. "I'm leaving, and I'm never coming back."

"Please don't go," said Ingjald. "I can't bear to see you leave."

"You can't sway me," said Oddr. "I'll not stay any longer."

"You can't sail a ship by yourself," said Ingjald. "Who will go with you? Where is your crew?"

"Asmund is coming with me," said Oddr. "We can sail just fine by ourselves."

"It's hard of you, Oddr, to leave me and take my son with you. Go away if you must, but let Asmund come back soon."

"Oh, Asmund won't come back any time before I do," said Oddr. "And besides, this serves you right for inviting that horrid old witch here when I told you I didn't want you to."

And so Ingjald gave Oddr and Asmund one of his ships, and when they had prepared for their voyage, he went down to the beach to see them off.

"Good luck to you," said Ingjald. "Good luck and a safe voyage. Maybe someday I will see you both again."

When Oddr and Asmund had said their own farewells to Ingjald, they pushed their ship out into the surf and rowed away. Ingjald watched them until they had rowed out of sight, and then he went back to his house.

## Örvar-Oddr in the Land of the Giants

One day, Oddr was traveling about and came to a steep cliff that overlooked a gorge. In the gorge was a river that was roaring along in cascading rapids. Oddr needed to get to the other side of the gorge, but he could see no way across. He decided to have a rest to think about what to do next. He had hardly sat down when something very large and very strong grabbed him about the shoulders and lifted him off the ground. A giant vulture had swooped down and snatched Oddr up in its talons, and now it was flying away with him.

The vulture flew a very long way. It sailed over the gorge and over the lands beyond. It sailed on across the sea until it came to an island that rose out of the sea in sheer cliffs. On a shelf of rock on the cliffside was the vulture's nest, and in the nest were several hungry chicks. The vulture dropped Oddr into the nest amongst the chicks, but Oddr remained unharmed because he was wearing his magic shirt that protected him from all injuries.

Now Oddr was in an even worse plight than he had been at the cliff's edge, for here the cliffs were absolutely sheer both above and below, and there was no way for him to climb out of his predicament. He looked over the edge of the nest and saw the sea churning below. For a moment, he thought about jumping from the nest into the water, but then thought better of it because the water was so very far away, and he had no idea in which direction he should swim to get to land or even how far away land might be. Oddr decided that for the moment he would conceal himself in a crevice near the nest and wait for an opportunity to escape.

Every day, the vulture flew away from the nest and came back with some sort of meat in its talons with which to feed its young. It brought every sort of animal and fish, and sometimes even human remains, which the chicks gobbled up greedily. Sometimes the vulture brought back cooked meat, which Oddr snatched away and ate himself.

One day, just after the vulture had dropped off several large, roasted oxen for its chicks to eat, Oddr saw a boat row up to the edge of the cliff. In the boat was a giant. The giant looked up to the place where the vulture's nest was and said, "There it is. That's the nest of that foul bird who keeps stealing my dinner. I had intended to feast well myself on the king's oxen, not provide a feast for others. Now I only need to figure out how to rid myself of this pest."

When Oddr heard the giant, he came out of his hiding place, killed all the chicks, and then stood up. He shouted down to the giant, "All your things are up here. I've been guarding them for you." Then he went back into the crevice to see what would happen.

The giant climbed up the side of the cliff, took the roasted oxen from the nest, and brought them down to his boat. Then he climbed back up to the nest and said, "Oi, little man! Where are you? Come out and talk to me. Don't be frightened; I'll take you away from this place."

Oddr came out of the crevice. The giant picked him up and then climbed back down the cliff and put Oddr into his boat.

The giant said to Oddr, "So, little friend, how do you think I should rid myself of that pest?"

"Set fire to the nest," said Oddr. "When the vulture returns and flies in close to see what is going on, its feathers will catch fire. That will weaken the brute, and then we can kill it."

And so Oddr and the giant put that plan into action. It didn't take long for the nest to start burning, and soon the vulture returned, just as Oddr expected it would. It flew too close to the flames, setting its feathers alight. Then Oddr swooped in and killed the vulture. When the creature was dead, Oddr cut off its beak and talons. He gave them to the giant, and then the giant carried Oddr back into his boat.

As the giant rowed away from the cliff, Oddr said, "What is your name?"

"I am called Hildir," said the giant. "I live in the Land of the Giants. My wife's name is Hildirid, and we have a daughter named Hildigunn. Just yesterday, my wife gave birth to a fine son, and we've named him Godmund. I have two brothers, named Ulf and Ylfing. We're getting ready to have a contest amongst ourselves to see which of us should be the king of the giants."

"How will the contest be decided?" said Oddr.

"Well, the one who has done the most heroic deed and whose dog wins the dogfight at the Assembly of Giants will be made king."

"Which of you do you think will win?" said Oddr.

"It won't be me, I can tell you that," said Hildir. "I've always lived in my brothers' shadows, and I don't expect that to change anytime soon."

"If you could win, would you want to be the king?" asked Oddr.

"Oh, yes, indeed, I'd love to be king," said Hildir, "but there's no way that will happen. Ulf is sure to enter his pet wolf into the dogfight, and it's never lost a fight yet; it's that strong and that savage. Ulf also went on a journey to a faraway land and brought back the head of a great catlike thing, with orange fur and black stripes. He says it's called a tiger, and that it's very fierce indeed."

"Ulf does sound like a tough competitor," said Oddr.

"Oh, Ulf is nothing to Ylfing," said the giant. "Ylfing's polar bear will make mincemeat of anything anyone cares to match it with in the dogfight, and Ylfing killed a unicorn the other day and brought back its head as evidence. I haven't done anything nearly as heroic. For that matter, I don't even own a dog."

"Yes, those do seem very difficult odds," said Oddr, "but maybe if a friend helped you, you could find a way around the problem."

The giant laughed. "Oh, you're a funny one, you are, although there's no denying you have good brains in that tiny head of yours. I think I'll give you as a present to Hildigunn. You'll make a fine toy for her, and she can take care of you and baby Godmund at the same time."

It took hardly any time for the giant to row his boat back to his home. When they arrived, Hildir showed Oddr to his daughter and said, "This little man is yours to play with. But mind you, you must treat him well! Treat him just as well as you would your baby brother."

Oddr looked up at Hildigunn. She was far from fully grown, but Oddr only came up to just above her knee, even though he was a very tall man indeed, and Hildigunn's father towered over her. Hildigunn picked up Oddr and began to dandle him on her knee. She sang:

*Little tiny man with down on your chin,*

*Baby Godmund is already bigger than you.*

Then Hildigunn took Oddr and lay him down in the cradle next to baby Godmund, and Oddr saw that he was indeed smaller even than the baby giant. For a little while, Hildigunn rocked the cradle and sang lullabies to Oddr and the baby, but eventually she decided that Oddr wasn't to sleep with Godmund but with her, so she picked Oddr up and placed him in her bed, where she hugged and kissed him all night. Oddr decided that the best strategy would be to play along with the giant girl and to wait for his chance to get away.

After a few days of playing whatever games Hildigunn asked him to play, Oddr said, "I know I seem very small indeed to you and that you think of me as a child, but among my own people, I am a grown man and am considered particularly large and strong. In fact, my people are a lot bigger and stronger than the other people who live near us, and we're better looking, too. But for all that, we're not any smarter than the other people are."

Now, the giant had rescued Oddr toward the end of the summer, and so Oddr stayed that winter with the giant family. When spring came, Oddr went to Hildir and said, "I know your assembly is coming up soon. What would you give me if I could find you a dog that could best all the other dogs at the fight there?"

"If someone could give me a dog that would win that fight, I'd give that person just about anything they asked for. Do you know where I might find such a dog?"

"I certainly do," said Oddr. "Do you know where the Vargey Islands are?"

"Yes, I know them, although I've never actually been there," said Hildir.

"Well, on those islands, there is a great creature called the brown bear. In the winter, it digs itself a den and sleeps and sleeps until spring. When spring comes, it comes out of its den and goes looking for food because it is quite famished after not having eaten for so long, and because it's so hungry, it's also very fierce and will kill and eat anything that crosses its path. It's not afraid of people at all; bears like that who live near farms will go right into the cattle pens, take a calf, and then run away with it to eat it in the forest. And if the farmer dares to get in the bear's way, well, the bear thinks that fresh farmer makes just as good a meal as fresh calf does. I think if you could find one of these bears, it probably would beat your brothers' dogs quite handily."

Hildir said, "Your story intrigues me. Tomorrow, I want you to help me catch one of these bears, and if I become king, I will reward you as generously as I can."

In the morning, as Hildir and Oddr were loading the giant's boat with supplies for their journey, Hildigunn came down to the beach and asked Oddr to step aside and have a word with her.

"Will you be coming back here when your business is done?" she said.

"I don't know," said Oddr. "But I think it rather unlikely."

"Oh, dear," said Hildigunn. "I do so wish you would come back. I love you so very much, despite your small stature. Also, you should know that I am expecting a child. There's no one else but you who could be the father, even though you're so small that one would think it impossible. But because I love you so much, I'll let you go wherever you want to go if that's what you want, but you should know that if I wanted to keep you here by force, I could most certainly do it. Instead, I'll just mourn your departure, because it's more important that you be happy than it is for you to stay here with me, and it seems to me that you don't want to stay. Now tell me, when the child is born, what shall I do with it?"

"If the child is a boy," said Oddr, "keep him with you until he is ten years old and then send him to me to be trained in the ways of men. But if the child is a girl, keep her here with you always and raise her yourself. I know you will do that very well, but I have no idea how to raise a girl myself."

Then Hildigunn said farewell to Oddr and went into the house, weeping bitterly. Oddr got into the boat, and the giant rowed them away from the shore.

Now, the giant was very strong and a very good rower, but even with calm seas, they were not making very fast progress. Oddr then decided he would use the luck of the men of Hrafnista to make their voyage go more swiftly. He hoisted a sail, and immediately a fair wind blew up. The ship leapt through the water, going twice as fast as it had been going with the giant at the oars.

The wind whipped up great waves that pitched the boat up and down. Hildir looked at the waves, and then he looked toward the shore, where it seemed that the land was jumping up and down of its own accord, which frightened Hildir greatly. Clinging to the gunwale for dear life, he went to where Oddr was standing, picked him up, and then slammed him down to the deck, pinning him there.

"I don't know how you're doing this thing," roared the giant, "but whatever witchcraft it is that makes the land jump about, stop it at once, or I will kill you and throw your carcass overboard for the fish to eat."

"What, have you never sailed before?" said Oddr. "This isn't witchcraft; it's just sailing. If you let me up, I can show you."

Hildir let Oddr stand up. Oddr lowered the sail, and immediately everything was calm.

"See?" said Oddr. "Now that we're not sailing with the wind, everything is calm. If we sail, we'll get to our destination faster, but there will be waves, and it will look like the land is jumping. You needn't worry, though; that's just what things look like when you sail. Can we try it again? We can always stop if it frightens you or if you need a rest."

Hildir agreed to let Oddr hoist the sail again now that he understood what was happening. He had also seen how much faster they had been traveling when the sail was up, and he was eager to get to the islands to catch a bear. Once the sail was up again, Hildir sat quietly near the boat's prow and let Oddr do all the work, and in no time they had arrived at the island where they were to look for a bear.

Not far from the beach was a mountain. At the base of the mountain was a great pile of scree. Oddr said, "I'll bet there's a bear in there under that scree. They like to make their dens in such places. Maybe you could put your hand in there to see what you'll find."

"That's a good idea," said Hildir, who pushed his great hand into the stones and began feeling about. When he had pushed his whole arm in right up to his shoulder, he stopped and said, "I think there's something here that might be a bear. I'm going to put on a glove before I try to grab it, though."

Hildir put on his glove and plunged his arm back into the scree. When he brought his arm back out, he was pulling a bear along by its ears. The bear was very angry at having been pulled out of its den early. It scratched and bit, and soon Hildir's hands were covered with cuts.

"You were right about how fierce this beast is," said Hildir. "What do I do now?"

"Take the bear home with you, and put it somewhere safe inside your house where no one can see it and where it can't get out. Don't feed it anything until after the dogfight. When it's time for your assembly, pit your bear against your brothers' dogs. If your bear doesn't win, then meet me back here at the same time next year so that I can give you something else to try."

"I'd like you to meet me here at this same spot next year whatever happens at the assembly," said the giant.

"Very well," said Oddr. "I will be here."

Then Hildir and Oddr said their farewells. Hildir set off for home in his boat with the bear, and Oddr went his own way.

As he had promised, Oddr returned to that place the following spring. He went a little way into the forest that was nearby, thinking that Hildir might want to kill him if the bear hadn't won the contest as Oddr said it would. Oddr didn't have long to wait before Hildir drew his boat up onto the beach. The giant took two chests and a great cauldron full of silver out of the boat and set them down in the place where he had promised to meet Oddr. Hildir waited for a while, but Oddr did not show himself. Hildir waited a little while more, then sighed and said, "Oddr, I do so wish you were here to take your reward. It's really not polite for you not to meet me here when you said you would. But I can't stay any longer. I can't leave my kingdom unguarded. Here are two chests filled with gold and a cauldron filled with silver. I'll put this big stone on top of them so that the wind can't take them away, and I'll put some other treasures here on top of the stone.

"Maybe you are waiting nearby and don't want to show yourself, so in case you can hear me: My dog bested all the others at the assembly, and when the people saw the beak and talons of that foul vulture that we killed last year, they decided I was the most valiant of all my brothers. I've been made king, and I've you to thank for it. If you ever decide to come and visit me, I'll treat you as a most honored guest. And I'd also like to let you know that Hildigunn had her baby. He's a fine boy, and we've named him Vignir. Hildigunn says that you're the father, but I'll raise him like he's my very own. I'll teach him all the things a boy should know, and when he's ten years old, we'll send him to you, as Hildigunn promised she would do."

Then the giant got back into his boat and rowed away. Oddr came out of his hiding place and saw that the giant had placed a sword, a helmet, and a shield on top of the stone. Oddr took those things off the great slab and then tried to push the stone aside, but it was so heavy that even with many strong men to help him, he would not be able to lift it. So Oddr took the weapons that the giant had left and felt very well recompensed indeed, for these were all very valuable treasures.

# The Voyages to Vinland

*The story of the attempted Viking settlement in what is now eastern Canada was the subject of much controversy for a very long time. Many scholars had doubted its historical veracity, but in 1960, the Norwegian archaeologist Anne Stine Ingstad and her husband Helge discovered the remains of what seemed to be a Viking settlement in L'Anse aux Meadows on the large island on the Gulf of St Lawrence in Newfoundland. At this site, which apparently was in use c. 990–1050 CE, Ingstad found the remains of several houses, everyday household items, the remains of a loom, an iron smithy, and rivets such as those that Vikings used to build their ships. While it is unlikely that this particular settlement is the one called "Leif's houses" in the saga, it provides incontrovertible proof of a Norse presence in North America around the turn of the eleventh century. Not only that, but more recent archaeological excavations, such as the one on Baffin Island in the Canadian province of Nunavut that began in 2001, have continued to turn up evidence of other Viking settlements.*

The Vinland Sagas *is the collective title given to* The Saga of Eirik the Red *and* The Saga of the Greenlanders, *each of which contain a version of the Norse sojourns in northeastern Canada. Although it is now generally accepted that Norse explorers did make relatively short-lived settlements in North America, it would be a mistake to take these thirteenth-century Norse texts as actual historical documents, not least because they contain elements that suggest a certain amount of romanticization of this new place the Norse called "Vinland," supposedly named after the great number of wild grapes that grew there. One such romanticized element concerns the harshness of the winters. The sagas report that the winters at the Vinland settlement were relatively mild, without much snow or freezing temperatures, but anyone who knows anything about northeastern Canadian weather will understand this to be more a product of wishful thinking (or perhaps an element of propaganda) than a description of actual winter conditions in that part of the world.*

*Despite their fictionalization of historical events,* The Vinland Sagas *remain vital documents in the history of both Europe and the Americas. In these sagas, we read of the first attempted European settlements in North America and the first contacts between Europeans and Indigenous Americans, and of the courage and resourcefulness of the Norse people who made voyages west to explore a new land.*

*Of Bjarni Herjolfsson*

Once there was a man named Bjarni Herjolfsson who was a well-respected merchant with his own ship. Bjarni's parents lived in Iceland. Sometimes Bjarni would spend his winters with them, while at other times he would spend them in Norway. Bjarni was an adventurous man, well willing to take risks to find new lands.

One summer, Bjarni's father, Herjolf, decided to leave Iceland and join Eirik the Red's new settlement in Greenland. Herjolf sold his farm, then put his family, slaves, and possessions into ships and sailed to Greenland, where he began a new farm at a place he called Herjolfsness. As he had been in Iceland, Herjolf was a well-respected and well-off man in Greenland as well.

Now, Herjolf moved to Greenland while Bjarni was away on a voyage. When Bjarni arrived at the port in Iceland, he went up to his father's farm to visit his parents, but he found the farmstead abandoned. Alarmed, Bjarni rushed over to a neighbor's house and asked what had become of his family. "Oh, they up and moved to Greenland, they did," said the neighbor. "Went to join old Eirik at that new colony of his."

Bjarni was pleased to find that nothing terrible had happened to his family in his absence, but now he had to decide whether to winter in Iceland or to go elsewhere. As he walked back to the port, he decided he would go and find his family and winter with them, as had been his custom on occasion. Bjarni arrived back at the ship, where his men had started unloading their cargo.

Bjarni said, "Stop unloading. We need to discuss what we're going to do. My father has moved to Greenland, so I'd like to go there to trade our goods and spend the winter. Who will come with me?"

The sailors all agreed that they'd go with Bjarni, even though none of them had ever sailed to Greenland before and only knew which direction to sail, but not exactly where Greenland lay.

As soon as the tide turned, Bjarni and his men sailed away from Iceland with a good, fair wind. They sailed for three days with this wind, and at the end of the third day, they were on the open ocean with no land in sight. It was then that their fortunes turned. The wind that had taken them this far shifted to the north, and thick fog descended all around them. They struck their sails to wait for the fog to dissipate, not wanting to lose their way at a time when the winds were against them and they could see nothing but the patch of sea on which their ship was bobbing.

Finally, the fog cleared, and the men were able to get their bearings. The wind was fair once more, so they hoisted the sail and continued their journey. After another day's sailing, they sighted land.

"Is this Greenland?" asked one of the sailors.

"I'm not sure," said Bjarni, "but I don't think it is. I don't know where we are."

"What shall we do now?" asked another sailor.

"Let's sail closer to that land and see what manner of place it is. Perhaps I am mistaken and it is Greenland indeed."

When the ship neared the coastline, Bjarni saw that they were in a strange land that neither he nor his men had ever seen before. Bjarni had heard people tell of Greenland, that it had many mountains and cliffs and glaciers, but this new land was nothing like that. The land was covered with thick forests that blanketed softly rolling hills, and there was no ice to be seen anywhere. Bjarni's ship had come fairly close to land when the wind failed.

"I say we put in here and take on firewood and water," said one sailor. "We don't know where we are, and who knows when we'll next have that chance?"

"No," said Bjarni. "We sail on. We have wood and water aplenty. We'll sail close to this coastline, and if need be, we can beach the ship farther on."

"This is folly," said one of the sailors. "We'll end up in the middle of the ocean with nothing to drink."

"Yes," said another. "We should put in here. It won't take us long, and we'll be glad we did later."

The other sailors agreed that this was the best plan, but Bjarni overruled them, and so they sailed on along this strange, new coastline. After a time, they came to a new place that was mountainous and covered with glaciers.

"Is this Greenland?" asked one of the sailors.

"I don't think so," said Bjarni. "From what I've heard, Greenland is a much more hospitable place than this. Let's sail on."

And so they sailed, hugging this new coastline, and soon they discovered that this place was a small island and not Greenland at all. They changed their course to leave the island behind them, setting out in the direction they thought best and with a good, fair wind.

Toward the end of the day, clouds rolled in, and a great storm began to blow around them. "Reef the sail!" said Bjarni. "Make sure the cargo is secure! We'll run before the storm, but I'll not have us lose our sail and rigging!"

It was a hard time and a dangerous one. The little ship was tossed on the waves, and the sail and rigging strained under the force of the wind. For four days the storm blew, but when it finally cleared, Bjarni and his men saw land on the horizon.

"Is this Greenland?" asked the sailors.

"I think it might be," said Bjarni, "but we'll need to sail closer."

They sailed on, and when they were close enough to see the features of the land, Bjarni said, "Yes, I think this is Greenland. This is the kind of place others have told me about. We'll beach the ship here. At the very least, we need to rest and take on water and other supplies before we go any farther."

As the ship approached the shore, they saw that another ship was already beached there before them. "This is a good sign," said Bjarni. "At the very least, we've come to a place where others make their homes. They'll be able to tell us where we are."

They beached the ship, and then Bjarni said, "I'm going to go in search of whoever lives here. Two of you come with me, and the rest stay here and see to repairs."

Bjarni and his companions walked inland, and soon they came to a prosperous farmstead. They knocked on the door of the farmhouse, and who should answer but Bjarni's own father!

"Bjarni! Welcome, my boy, and welcome to your friends!" said Bjarni's father. "We hadn't thought to see you for another year at least. Come in, come in, and tell me and your mother how you have fared."

Bjarni was delighted to have reached Greenland at last, and he was even more delighted that the first Greenlanders he met were his very own family. Bjarni and his men took some refreshment and spoke for a while with Bjarni's parents, but they did not stay long.

"I need to go back to my ship to let my men know that we have come to a safe port and can begin trading," said Bjarni. "I'll come back as soon as my business is done and spend the winter here with you, if I may."

Bjarni's family said that he was more than welcome, and they offered to find lodgings for his men as well. Bjarni and his friends went back to their ship in high spirits, and when all their cargo had been sold and the profits fairly divided, they went their own ways to the places where they were to spend the winter.

When the spring came, Bjarni's father said, "So, my boy, are you taking to the sea again? What do you plan to do next?"

"I've had enough of voyaging," said Bjarni. "I'd like to stay here and help you with the farm, if that suits you and Mother."

"Of course!" said Bjarni's father. "You are more than welcome here. We're very glad you've come home to us."

And so it was that Bjarni gave up his life of voyaging and stayed on his father's farm. Bjarni took the farm over when Herjolf died, but he never forgot the new lands he had seen rising out of the sea, far from Greenland's shores.

### *Of Leif Eiriksson*

One time after he had ended his trading voyages, Bjarni Herjolfsson sailed to Norway to visit Earl Eirik Hakonarson. The earl was delighted to have Bjarni as a guest, and he listened with great interest to Bjarni's tale of his adventure to the west of Greenland, but because Bjarni could not give a greater description of the country he had found, many people thought that he had lacked both courage and curiosity and thought less of him for that. For his part, the earl thought that Bjarni had done well, and made Bjarni a retainer at his court. Bjarni spent the winter in Norway with Earl Eirik and then returned to Greenland in the summer.

Word spread quickly of Bjarni's adventure. Many people wondered whether it would be possible to find those lands again and maybe even make a new settlement there. Leif, the son of Eirik the Red, heard Bjarni's tale and decided that he would try his own luck at finding that place to see whether it might be fit to settle.

Leif went to Herjolfsness to visit Bjarni. "I'd like to buy your ship," said Leif. "And I want to hear all about your adventure. I'm gathering men and supplies for a journey to that place, and it will help me if you can tell me all you know."

Bjarni readily agreed to sell his ship and tell Leif everything he could about his journey. When that business was accomplished, Leif sent word that he was seeking a crew for this adventure. He hired thirty-five men to sail with him.

When everything was ready, Leif went to his father and said, "I'm ready to leave for that new land Bjarni found. Will you come with me and help lead the expedition?"

"I'm honored to be asked, my son," said Eirik, "but I am an old man now. Sailing is a nasty, cold, wet, uncomfortable business, and I no longer have the strength for it. Your journey is a job for young men like yourself."

"Oh, come now, Father," said Leif. "You're not as old and weak as you seem. I'm sure the voyage would do you good, and it will help to have someone of your stature as part of our expedition. It will bring us luck."

In the end, Eirik agreed to join the adventure, but on the day they were to embark, Eirik was thrown from his horse on the way to the port. Eirik's leg was badly injured.

"This is a sign that I am not to go with you," said Eirik. "I should stay here. That is to be my fate."

And so Eirik went back to his homestead, and Leif commanded the journey alone.

Leif and his crew finished their preparations and set sail. It was not many days before they sighted land to the west. "This must be the land Bjarni spoke of," said Leif. "We will sail closer and then go ashore to see what may be seen."

They sailed closer to the land until they found a good place to drop their anchor. Then Leif took a party of men with him and rowed ashore. When they arrived on the land, they saw that it was mostly flat rock and glaciers. "This cannot be the land that Bjarni told us of," said Leif. "This is no place for a settlement. We'll go back to the ship and then sail on. But we have done better than Bjarni did, for we came ashore to see what we might find. Since all we found were stone and ice, I shall call this place Helluland [Stone-slab Land]."

Leif and his men returned to their ship. They set sail again, moving down the coast until they came to a different land, one that was not all rock and ice. As before, they sailed close to the shore and dropped their anchor. Leif chose a party of men to go ashore with him. They rowed onto the beach, which was made of fine white sand. Leif and his men walked inland. They found that the land was relatively flat and had many dense forests. "We will call this place Markland [Forest Land]," said Leif. "But we won't stay here. Let's sail on and see what else we might find."

Leif and his crew sailed for two days before they sighted another shore. This time, they had arrived at an island. They went ashore and walked through the dewy grass. The men collected the dew in their hands and tasted it.

"This is so good!" said one man.

"Yes!" said another. "Even at home the dew is not as sweet."

They explored the island for a while longer, then returned to their ship and sailed around the island, which was not far from a much greater land. They sailed into the sound between the island and the headland that lay to their north, then rounded the headland. There they met with their first real difficulty: The water here was very shallow, and so when the tide lowered, the ship was left stranded on the sand.

"I don't want to wait here," said Leif. "We should go ashore anyway. We have plenty of time before the tide changes and we can sail once more."

Leif and his men walked to the shore, bringing rowboats with them. There they found a river that flowed to the sea, and by following the river, they soon came to a lake.

"This is a good place," said Leif. "Let's go back to the ship. When the tide lifts it, we can row upriver and drop anchor in the lake."

As soon as the water was deep enough, Leif and his crew rowed their ship up the river and into the lake, where they dropped their anchor. They took their bedrolls and other supplies to the shore, where they built shelters out of stone and turf. They took their fishing gear and caught many fine salmon, which were plentiful both in the lake and in the river.

"Look at this beast!" said one man, holding up a huge salmon he had just caught. "Have you ever seen its like? Even at home we have no such salmon as this. Tonight, we eat well!"

It wasn't long until Leif and his men decided that they would spend the winter there to see what it was like. They built proper houses for themselves since the shelters would not be sufficient for the colder weather.

When winter came, the explorers were pleased to find that it was much less cold than at home, and the grass was still good for cattle to graze. Although the nights lengthened and the days shortened as the solstice approached, the sun still rose and was in the sky for part of the day, unlike at home, where both days and nights were dark at that time.

Once the houses were built, Leif explained how they were to go about exploring the land. "Every day, we will split up into two groups. One group stays here with the houses. The other group goes exploring. But the explorers must be able to return to the houses before sunset, and no one must leave the group for any reason."

This was how they lived for some time. On some days, Leif would stay with the houses, while on other days he went with the explorers. One day, Leif stayed at the houses, while the others went out to scout the land. The exploration party returned to the houses, but one of the explorers was missing, a German man by the name of Tyrkir, who was a great friend of Eirik the Red's and who had been Leif's foster-father when he was a boy.

"Where is Tyrkir?" Leif demanded of the explorers. "You knew you weren't supposed to let anyone separate from the group. I need to be able to trust all of you to follow orders, and this day you have not."

Leif then chose twelve men to accompany him to look for Tyrkir, but they had not gone far before Tyrkir appeared.

"Tyrkir!" Leif shouted. "Thank the gods you are safe. Where have you been?"

Tyrkir replied with a flood of rapid German that none of the others understood. The older man seemed very excited about something, hardly able to contain himself.

"Slow down, foster-father," said Leif. "Slow down, and speak Norse. We don't understand you at all."

Tyrkir took a deep breath, then replied in Norse. "Grapes! Grapes and grapevines! Whole fields of them!"

"Are you sure?" said Leif.

"Very sure," said Tyrkir. "Where I come from, they grow many grapes. I know what grapes and grapevines look like. Come, I'll show you."

Leif saw that the shadows were lengthening and that night was not far off. "No, we'll not go now," he said. "It's too close to nightfall.

Let's go back to the houses and have a meal. We'll go to the grapevines in the morning."

When the sun rose, Leif gathered all the men together. "Here is what we will do. We will cut grapes and grapevines to take home, and also a load of timber. Then we'll go back to Greenland and tell everyone what we have found in this new place. We will call it Vinland [Wine Land] since it has such an abundance of grapes and grapevines."

The men agreed that this was the best course to take, and so they began doing the work that Leif had suggested they do.

When spring came, they made everything ready to sail home. The ship was laden with grapes, vines, and timber, and the men were well pleased with what they had found. They had a fair wind and a sunny day when they departed Vinland, and everyone was in high spirits.

They sailed on for a time, with Leif at the rudder. Suddenly he changed course, commanding that the sails be brought in tight.

"Why do we sail so close to the wind?" asked one of the men. "This surely is folly. We'll never get home if we sail like this."

"Look out to sea, over there," said Leif. "Tell me what you see."

The man looked and said, "There's nothing there." Others of the crew looked and also said they saw nothing.

"I think there's a ship over there, or maybe a skerry," said Leif. "Look more closely."

The crew looked and agreed that there must be a skerry, but none of them understood why Leif would care about a bit of rock out in the middle of the sea.

"It's not just a bit of rock," said Leif. "I think there are people there. And if there are people there, they will need our help."

"Pirates, like as not," said one of the men. "We'll sail up to them, and then they'll board us and we'll have to fight for our lives."

"Be that as it may," said Leif, "we still have the advantage of them. And it would be a shameful thing to sail past without seeing whether they are friendly and in need of help or not."

They sailed as close to the skerry as they could and then dropped their anchor. Then Leif and a few other men lowered the rowboat into the water and rowed over to the skerry, where they found a group of fourteen men and one woman together on the rock with a pile of the cargo and belongings they had managed to save before their ship sank.

"Thank the gods you've come!" said one man. "We thought we had met our doom for sure."

"Which of you is the captain?" said Leif.

"I am," said another.

"What is your name?" asked Leif.

"I am Thorir, and I come from Norway. What is your name?"

"My name is Leif."

"Not Eirik's son, Eirik the Red of Brattahild in Greenland?" said Thorir.

"The very same," said Leif. "Come aboard my ship and I'll take you to Greenland, where you are welcome to stay or to find another ship to take you home. We'll bring as much of your cargo and belongings as my ship can hold, but the rest will have to stay here."

Thorir and his wife, Gudrid, and the others readily agreed to Leif's offer. They boarded Leif's ship with a good portion of their belongings and cargo, then sailed back to Brattahild, where Leif and his crew unloaded their ship.

"Won't you spend the winter with me and my father?" said Leif to Thorir and Gudrid. "I'll also see to it that your friends have lodgings so that no one goes without shelter."

Leif was as good as his word. He found lodgings for the thirteen men who he had rescued along with Thorir and Gudrid, and he also made sure his crew had places to go for the winter. When everyone saw what a wealth of timber and grapes Leif had brought back, and when they heard his tale of his sojourn in Vinland and the rescue of Thorir and his friends, they began calling Leif "the Lucky," since he had had so much good fortune on that journey.

The winter was not as gentle as the summer had been. Thorir and his crew all fell sick, and most of them died, including Thorir. The sickness did not spare Leif's family either, for his father, Eirik, also fell ill and died at that time.

## Of Thorvald Eiriksson

Leif's adventure in Vinland was the talk of Greenland. Leif's brother, Thorvald, listened carefully to the stories and thought long about them. Finally he decided that he would try his own luck in the new land. He bought a ship and raised a crew of thirty after hearing all Leif had to tell about how to get to Vinland and where he had set up the houses. When the ship was provisioned and the crew ready, Thorvald set sail to Vinland and arrived at Leif's camp after an uneventful voyage.

They beached their ship and brought their provisions ashore. They made the houses ready and explored a little bit of the land around the camp. At the end of the day, Thorvald told his crew, "We will spend the winter here, and in the spring we will see what else this land has to offer."

The crew agreed that this was a good plan. They settled in for the winter and lived on the salmon that teemed in the river and the lake.

In the spring, Thorvald and his crew worked to repair the ship. When summer came, Thorvald sent a party of men in the ship's boat to explore the land to the west of them. The men explored along the coast throughout the summer, and when they returned that autumn, they had much to tell Thorvald and the others.

"The land is very fair," said the leader of the expedition. "There are thick forests and beaches of fine white sand. To the north, there are many small islands, and the sea in that place is quite shallow. We saw no other people, and no animals to speak of, the entire time we were on our journey.

"After we had explored the coast for a while, we rowed over to the islands. We found much the same there as we had on the headland, although we did find one thing made of wood that looked like what we use to cover stores of grain. That certainly was made by human hands, but we did not find the people who made it or any other signs of them."

The following summer, Thorvald and his crew decided to sail in the ship to the east to see what they might find there, leaving part of their number behind to keep watch over the houses. But Thorvald's new journey was not as fortunate as the one his men had made with the small boat the summer before. A storm blew up as Thorvald's ship rounded one headland. The wind and the waves drove the ship onto the rocks, cracking the keel. The men managed to get the ship safely onto the beach, and no lives were lost, but there was to be no more exploring for a long time because the ship had taken such heavy damage.

The men worked for many days putting in a new keel and repairing the sides of the ship. When they were finished, Thorvald said, "Let's set that broken keel up in a place of honor here. We'll call this place Kjalarnes [Keel Point]."

As soon as the ship was completely seaworthy, Thorvald and his men resumed their journey eastward along the coast. There they found some fjords and a cape that extended northward toward the sea. They beached their ship at the mouth of one of the fjords, and all went ashore. When they had walked some way inland, Thorvald looked about him and was very pleased by what he saw. "I think I shall settle here," he said. "This is a very fair place, indeed."

They returned to the ship, but one of Thorvald's companions looked along the beach and said, "Wait. Look there. What do you see?"

"I see three humps on the sand," said another of the men.

"Those weren't there before," said the first. "And I don't think they are part of the landscape."

"We'll divide into three groups," said Thorvald. "We'll go silently up to those humps, whatever they are, and deal with what we find there. Each group takes one hump. Ready? Let's go."

As Thorvald and his men crept closer, they saw that the humps were three small boats with skin coverings. They flipped the boats over, and under each one they found three men hiding. One man managed to escape in his boat, but Thorvald and his crew killed all the others.

Thorvald and his men then looked about them and saw what looked like hills farther down the fjord. "I don't think those are hills," said Thorvald. "I think those must be dwellings of some kind. Those nine men didn't just appear out of thin air."

The day had been a long and strenuous one. Thorvald and his men were exhausted. They lay down to rest right where they were, and soon all of them had fallen into a deep sleep. They did not awaken until they heard the sound of a voice calling to them. "Wake up!" cried the voice. "Wake up, Thorvald! Wake up all you sailors! Board your ship now if you value your lives! Wake up!"

The men all sprang up and looked down the fjord. Hundreds of skin boats like the ones they had found were now being paddled toward them, and every boat was full of fierce-looking warriors.

"Back to the ship!" cried Thorvald. "Back to the ship, and set the war shields on the gunwales as soon as may be. We will defend ourselves as well as we can, but try not to fight back if it isn't needed."

The men set the shields on the gunwales as the warriors in the boats rowed ever closer. The warriors had bows with them, and soon a hail of arrows was flying toward Thorvald and his companions, who sheltered behind the shields. After a time, the attacking warriors stopped shooting, then turned their boats around and paddled away.

"Is anyone hurt?" asked Thorvald.

All the men replied that they had taken no injuries.

"I was not so fortunate," said Thorvald. "One of those arrows managed to fly between two of the shields. It pierced my armpit." Thorvald showed the arrow to his friends. "I fear this wound will be the death of me. Take me back to the place that I thought so fair, and bury me there, with a cross at my head and a cross at my feet. Call that place Krossanes [Cross Point] when I am laid to rest as I asked." Thorvald then died, and his friends buried him with the crosses at his head and feet as he had asked, because Thorvald was a Christian.

When Thorvald had been properly laid to rest, the men took ship and sailed back to the houses. They had much to tell their companions who had stayed behind, and their companions had much to tell them. They decided to spend the winter there at the houses and sail back to Greenland in the spring, having laid in a cargo of grapes and grapevines.

Spring came, and the men sailed safely back to Greenland with a heavily laden ship. They steered their boat into the port at Eiriksfjord and were welcomed home with much joy by their friends and families. They met with Leif and told him all that had happened on their journey, and their tale was not a short one.

### *Of Thorstein Eiriksson*

Eirik the Red had a third son who was named Thorstein. Thorstein married Gudrid, the widow of Thorir, who had been rescued along with her late husband and their ship's crew by Thorstein's brother, Leif. Thorstein wanted to go to Vinland to fetch the body of his brother, so that he might be laid in his own native soil rather than rest in a foreign land. Thorstein gathered a crew of twenty-five large, strong men, and put to sea with them and with his wife, Gudrid.

Thorstein's adventure went ill from the very beginning. Thorstein and his crew sailed to and fro on the open ocean, not able to find their way until winter was already settling in. "We can't find our way, and soon it will be too cold to sail," said Thorstein. "We'll return to Greenland and wait out the winter, and then try again when the warmer weather comes."

And so they sailed to Greenland, and they put in at Lysefjord, a settlement in the west. When they arrived, Thorstein arranged winter lodgings for all his crew, but was unable to find a place for himself and his wife, for Christianity had only lately come to Greenland. They camped on the beach next to their ship for two nights. On the day after the second night, some men came to Thorstein's tent. "Who is there inside the tent?" they asked.

"There are two of us here," said Thorstein. "Who is asking?"

One of the men said, "My name is also Thorstein, but I am also known as Thorstein the Black. I have come to ask you to spend the winter with me in my home."

"That is a generous offer," said Thorstein Eiriksson, "but first I must ask my wife whether she agrees."

Thorstein Eiriksson asked Gudrid what she thought of the offer.

"If you think it acceptable," she said, "then we should accept."

Thorstein Eiriksson said to the men outside the tent, "My wife agrees, and we gladly accept your offer of hospitality."

"That is good," said Thorstein the Black. "I will come back tomorrow to fetch you and your belongings. I can't promise that it will be a merry winter, for both my wife Grimhild and I are very staid and set in our ways, and I prefer my own company. We also have a different religion from you, but it seems to me that yours is better than mine."

The next day, Thorstein the Black came to the beach as promised. He helped Thorstein Eiriksson and Gudrid load their belongings onto his cart, and then drove them and their things back to his home. Thorstein the Black and his wife were very generous to their guests, and provided well for them throughout the winter.

Gudrid acquitted herself well in the house of her hosts. She was a very beautiful woman, and also a wise one who knew how to behave with strangers.

The winter had barely begun in earnest when an illness struck Lysefjord. Many of Thorstein Eiriksson's crew fell ill, and some of them died.

"Do not lay the bodies of my crew to rest here," said Thorstein Eiriksson. "I wish to take them back home to Eiriksfjord for burial when the summer comes."

The home of Thorstein the Black was not spared from the plague either. Grimhild fell ill, even though she was a large woman and just as strong as a man. Thorstein Eiriksson fell ill soon after Grimhild, and Grimhild died soon after that.

When Grimhild was dead, her husband said, "I am going out to find a plank to lay her body upon."

"Don't be too long, dear Thorstein," said Gudrid.

"I shan't tarry," said Thorstein, and then he left the room.

After Thorstein the Black had gone, Thorstein Eiriksson said, "Why is Grimhild behaving that way? She is pushing herself up on her elbow. She is trying to get out of bed and trying to find her shoes."

Just then, Thorstein the Black returned with a plank to lay his wife's body on, and the body of Grimhild fell back onto the bed with such force that every beam in the house creaked.

Thorstein the Black made a good coffin for his wife and laid her gently in it. When the coffin had been sealed, Thorstein the Black took it out of the house for burial. This took all the effort he could muster, even though he was a very strong man, for Grimhild was a very large and very strong woman.

The sorrows of that household were not yet over, for soon Thorstein Eiriksson also died. Gudrid and Thorstein the Black were there at his bedside when he gave up the ghost, and Gudrid was sorely grieved that her husband was no more.

Thorstein the Black was moved to pity by Gudrid's weeping. He picked her up and held her on his lap as he would a small child, and spoke words of comfort and encouragement to her. He also promised that Thorstein Eiriksson's body would be taken back to Eiriksfjord with the bodies of his crew, so that they all could be laid to rest together in the place that was their home. Thorstein the Black also told Gudrid that he would find other people to join them in his house so that she might be less lonely.

"Thank you, dear friend," said Gudrid. "I am grateful for your help and comfort."

Just then, the body of Thorstein Eiriksson sat up in the bed. "Where is Gudrid?" it asked.

Gudrid did not answer, and neither did Thorstein the Black.

The body of Thorstein Eiriksson asked twice more, "Where is Gudrid?"

Gudrid said to Thorstein the Black, "Should I answer it?"

"No, do not answer," he replied. "I will speak for you."

Then Thorstein the Black went over to the bed and knelt beside it. "Tell me what you want, dearest friend and bearer of my name. I am here."

For a moment, there was silence. Then the corpse spoke. "I have a message for Gudrid. I know what her fate is, and I want to tell her of myself so that she might not mourn so heavily. I have gone to a very good place where I shall rest well. Hear me, Gudrid, for what I say is true: You will marry an Icelander, and together you will have a long life and many children, all of them good and strong and sweet. You and your husband will leave Greenland and go to Norway for a time, and after that you will settle in Iceland, which will become your home. After your husband dies, you will make a pilgrimage to Rome. When you return to Iceland, a church will be built on your farm there, and you will take the holy vows of a nun. There you will stay until your death."

Then the body of Thorstein Eiriksson fell back on the bed. His body was prepared for burial and taken to his ship.

Thorstein the Black kept all the promises he had made to Gudrid. When the spring came, he sold his farm and his livestock. Then he took Gudrid and all her belongings to the ship where her husband's body lay, then sailed back to Eiriksfjord, where he saw to it that Thorstein Eiriksson and all his companions were laid to rest in the Christian churchyard as was right and proper for men of their faith.

Gudrid went to live with her brother-in-law Leif at Brattahild, while Thorstein the Black made his home in Eiriksfjord. Thorstein lived there for the rest of his days, and he was well respected by everyone for his generous spirit.

### *Of Thorfinn Karlsefni*

The summer that Thorstein Eiriksson was laid to rest in Eiriksfjord, a very wealthy man named Thorfinn Karlsefni came to Iceland from Norway. Thorfinn lodged with Leif Eiriksson the following winter, and soon he fell in love with Gudrid, the widow of Thorstein Eiriksson. One day, Thorfinn went to Gudrid and said, "I find that I love you very much, and would be honored if you would be my wife."

"I cannot answer now," said Gudrid, "but I will let you know soon."

Gudrid then went to her brother-in-law and told him of Thorfinn's proposal. "I would rather you answered Thorfinn on my behalf," said Gudrid.

"Do you approve of Thorfinn?" asked Leif. "Are you willing to marry him?"

"I am," said Gudrid. "He seems to be a good man."

Then Leif went to Thorfinn and told him that Gudrid accepted his proposal. They were wed later that same winter.

Now, Leif had been home from his voyage to Vinland for some time, but everyone still spoke of his adventures, and of the adventures of Thorvald and his crew. Many people urged Thorfinn to try his luck in Vinland. Thorfinn's wife, Gudrid, was among those.

Finally Thorfinn agreed. He hired a crew of sixty men and five women. They agreed to split the profits from the voyage equally among them. They also gathered livestock to take with them since they wanted to settle permanently in Vinland if possible.

Thorfinn went to Leif and said, "As you know, I am planning a voyage to Vinland. May I have the houses you built there?"

"I will gladly lend them to you," said Leif, "but I will not give them to you to be your own."

Thorfinn agreed to these terms and set sail as soon as he had a fair wind. It did not take long for his ships to arrive in Vinland. Everyone went ashore and set their bedding inside the houses. They then set their livestock free to look for pasturage and went looking for food for themselves. It did not take long for them to find good things to eat, for a rorqual had beached itself not far from the houses. The rorqual was still fresh, so Thorfinn and his crew butchered it. They ate very well that night and for many days afterward, and the animals found good grazing a little way inland from the houses. Soon the male animals became very restless and difficult to handle, not least the bull they had brought with them.

Once they had settled in, Thorfinn said, "Let us fell much timber now and leave it out to dry. We can take it back with us next summer and make a good profit from it."

This was done, and soon they had a good load of timber laid out on some stones. They also worked at gathering grapes, fishing in the river, and hunting game, both for their food at that time and to store away for the winter that was fast approaching.

When the warm weather came after their first winter at the houses, they had their first encounter with the people who were native to that land. A group of men carrying bundles of furs came out of the forest very close to the cattle pasture. The arrival of the strangers angered the bull, who snorted and pawed the ground at them. The native men had never seen a bull before. They were very frightened and ran to Thorfinn's house to get away from the angry animal.

The native men begged to be allowed into the house, but Thorfinn would not let them enter. For some time, Thorfinn and the native men shouted at one another, but since they did not understand each other's language, this was of no avail. Finally the men set their bundles of furs down on the ground in front of the houses and waited for Thorfinn and the others to come out to them.

When Thorfinn and his crew saw that the men had come to trade, they went out to greet them and see what they might exchange for the furs. The native men were greatly interested in the weapons and tools that Thorfinn and his crew had brought with them, but Thorfinn forbade trading anything made of metal. The Icelanders decided to see whether the native men would accept a gift of milk from the cows in exchange for the furs. The native people were greatly pleased with the milk. They drank all that Thorfinn's company gave them, then headed back to their own homes, leaving their furs and skins behind in exchange for the milk.

Once the native people had gone, Thorfinn said, "We need to be prepared to defend ourselves. Let us cut timber and build a palisade around our farm in case the native people become hostile."

Not long after the visit of the native men, Gudrid gave birth to a fine son. Thorfinn and Gudrid named him Snorri.

Early the next winter, the native men returned to Thorfinn's settlement, bearing bundles of furs and skins. When Thorfinn saw this, he said, "Milk the cows, and bring the milk out to the men in exchange for the furs. Do not give them anything else."

When the native men saw the cows being milked, they tossed their bundles over the palisade wall.

Now, while this was going on, Gudrid was sitting just inside the doorway of one of the houses, tending her little son, Snorri. While she rocked Snorri in his cradle, a shadow fell across the doorway. Gudrid looked up, and there she saw a strange woman. The woman was very short and had enormous eyes. She wore a tunic that closely fitted her body and a scarf over her hair. The strange woman came inside the doorway and asked, "What is your name?"

Gudrid replied, "My name is Gudrid. What is your name?"

"I am also Gudrid," said the strange woman.

Just as Thorfinn's wife was about to offer the stranger a place to sit, there was a loud crash as of thunder, and the strange woman disappeared. At the same time this happened, one of Thorfinn's men killed one of the natives for trying to steal weapons. The other natives then ran away, leaving all their goods behind. When Gudrid asked the others whether they had seen the strange woman, everyone said they had not.

Later that day, Thorfinn gathered all his crew together. He said to them, "I doubt the native people will leave us in peace much longer. We killed one of their own, and it's likely that they will be hostile when they come back. We need to have a plan for what to do when that happens. This is what we will do: Ten men will go to that headland over there and let themselves be seen by the natives. The rest of us will take our cattle into the forest, where we will cut a clearing for them. When they come at us through the forest, we will loose the bull on them before attacking them ourselves."

The others agreed to this plan. They chose a place with the lake on one side and the forest on the other to make the clearing.

It did not take long before a large group of native men came to where Thorfinn and the others waited with the cattle. There was a fight, and many of the native men were killed. One of the native men was very tall and good-looking; Thorfinn thought that this must be the chief of that people. Another of the native men found an axe that had been dropped during the fight. He looked at it for a moment, then swung it at one of his companions, killing him on the spot. The tall, handsome man grabbed the axe away from the one who had found it, and threw it as far as he could into the lake. Then all the native men ran away from that place, and troubled Thorfinn and his companions no more.

Thorfinn and the others spent another winter there, but when spring came, Thorfinn said, "I won't stay here any longer. I think we should all go back to Greenland. Let's load our ships with the timber and other good things that we can sell at home, and call an end to this adventure."

The others agreed that this was the best plan. They loaded their ships with the timber they had cut and with many grapevines and fine pelts. They set sail as soon as everything was ready, and after an uneventful voyage, they arrived safely at Eiriksfjord, where they spent the winter.

The following summer, Thorfinn readied his ship to sail to Norway. He had fair winds and arrived there after a brief voyage. He and his wife stayed in Norway for the winter, and they made a fair profit on the goods they had brought back from Vinland. The nobles of that place were very impressed with Thorfinn and Gudrid, and treated the two very well the whole time they were there.

In the spring, Thorfinn and Gudrid sailed for Iceland. They landed at Skagafjord, and when the ship had been brought ashore and secured against the winter weather, they went to Glaumbaer, where they bought land, built a house, and began to farm. Everyone in Glaumbaer and the surrounding lands were pleased that Thorfinn had come to settle among them, for he was thought to be a very fine man of good reputation. He and his wife had many children. They were a happy family and beloved of all their neighbors.

When Thorfinn died, Gudrid ran the farm herself. Snorri, her son who had been born in Vinland, helped her in this. Snorri found himself a good woman to be his wife, and they were soon wed. After the wedding, Gudrid went to Snorri and said, "You are a man full grown, with a beautiful wife who is a good woman. I give you this farm to be your own, for I am now going to go on a pilgrimage. I hope to go all the way to Rome. I wish all good blessings on you, on your wife, and on your children who are yet to come."

After Gudrid had left on her pilgrimage, Snorri had a church built there in Glaumbaer, and when Gudrid returned, she took vows as a nun and lived a monastic life at the church.

Thorfinn and Gudrid's children did very well for themselves, and were blessed, as Gudrid had said they would be. Snorri's son Thorgeir had a daughter named Yngveld, and her son Brand became a bishop. Snorri's daughter Hallfrid married a man named Runolf, and their son Thorlak also became a bishop. Snorri's brother, Bjorn, had a daughter named Thorunn, and her son, named Bjorn like his father, also became a bishop.

Thorfinn Karlsefni's family was very large and very prosperous. Everyone respected them, and they had a large number of descendants. It was Thorfinn who told most of the stories about these voyages, the tales of which have now been set down in writing.

### *Of Freydis Eiriksdottir*

On the day that Thorfinn, Gudrid, and their crew returned from Vinland, their ships sitting low in the water beneath loads of timber and other good things, the people of Eiriksfjord once again began talking of voyaging west to seek their own fortunes.

During that summer, two men from Norway arrived in Greenland. Their names were Helgi and Finnbogi, and they were brothers. They had been born in Iceland, in the Eastfjords. They found lodging and spent the winter in Greenland.

Now, Eirik the Red had a daughter named Freydis, and she lived at Gardar with her husband, Thorvard. She had heard of the two men from Norway and had been harboring thoughts of her own about a voyage to Greenland. Freydis went to the place where Helgi and Finnbogi were staying, and asked them whether they would like to be partners with her in a voyage to Vinland.

"We'll take your ship and mine," she said, "and whatever profits we make we will split equally among us."

"This is acceptable," said the brothers, and so the three of them began planning their voyage together.

Freydis went to her brother, Leif, and said, "Give me the houses that you have built in Vinland."

Leif replied, "I'll not give them to you, but you may borrow them for as long as you need them."

Freydis agreed with Helgi and Finnbogi that they would each take thirty men and some women with them aboard their ships. Freydis broke her word almost immediately by taking five extra men, concealing them aboard her ship until they arrived in Vinland, when it was too late to do anything about it.

Now, they agreed to sail together in convoy, and so the ships were never very far apart from one another, but Helgi's and Finnbogi's ship managed to arrive some time before Freydis's. When she disembarked, she found that Helgi and Finnbogi and their crews had begun putting away their belongings in some of the houses.

When Freydis arrived with her crew and their belongings, she saw what Helgi and Finnbogi had done. "Why have you moved into these houses with all your belongings?" she asked.

"We had an agreement," said Helgi. "We get to stay in the houses too, as we discussed before we left."

"No, we didn't agree to that, and neither did my brother," said Freydis. "Leif lent these houses to me, not to you. Pack up your things and get out. Build your own houses somewhere else."

"This is a wicked thing you do, Freydis," said Helgi. "Finnbogi and I would never stoop to such things."

And so Helgi, Finnbogi, and their crews went inland a little way and built a large house on the shore of the lake. While the brothers were building their house, Freydis ordered her crew to begin felling trees to make a cargo of timber.

When winter came, the brothers went to Freydis and said, "We should visit one another's houses during the winter. We can play games and make merry, just as we do at home at this time of the year."

Freydis agreed, but it did not take long before quarrels broke out between Freydis's people and the brothers' crews. The two groups stopped visiting one another, and so Helgi and Finnbogi's plan for a merry winter came to naught.

One morning, Freydis awoke very early while everyone else in the house was asleep. She got out of bed without waking her husband, got dressed, and put on her husband's cloak, but she did not put on any shoes. The grass was heavy with dew at that time. Freydis walked through the wet grass to the brothers' house. There she found the door ajar. She pushed it open and waited in the doorway. Finnbogi saw her standing there. From his bed at the other end of the house, he said, "What do you want, Freydis?"

"Come outside and talk to me," she said.

Finnbogi agreed. They went over to the trunk of a fallen tree and sat down for their talk.

"Are things well with you?" asked Freydis.

"Yes," said Finnbogi. "This country is a very agreeable place, and I'm glad I came. But it is a sorrowful thing that there is such ill feeling between us and between our crews."

"I agree," said Freydis, "but that is not why I have come to speak with you. I have come to ask that you exchange ships with me. Your ship is larger than mine, and I want to leave this place."

"Very well," said Finnbogi. "There's probably no point in denying you. I will trade you my ship for yours."

Then Finnbogi went back to his bed, and Freydis walked back to the houses, where everyone was still asleep. Freydis climbed into bed next to her husband, but because her feet were so wet and cold from her walk through the dew, it woke him up.

"Hey, there!" said Thorvard. "Why are your feet so cold and wet?"

"I went to visit Helgi and Finnbogi. I wanted to trade my ship for theirs. My request made them very angry, and they beat me and called me foul names. You likely won't do anything about it. Everyone knows you're a coward, and you probably won't stand up for me. It's too bad we're not in Greenland; my brothers would definitely do something about this insult. But since we're not in Greenland, all I can do is tell you that if you don't avenge me, I'll divorce you on the spot."

Thorvard was ashamed by what Freydis had said, and became angry. He woke the men of the house and told them to get their weapons and follow him. Thorvard, Freydis, and the others went to Helgi and Finnbogi's house, where Thorvard and his men took prisoner all the men who were inside. When they were all tied up outside the house, Thorvard said, "What do we do with them now?"

"Kill them," said Freydis.

"All of them?" asked Thorvard.

"Yes," said Freydis. "It's the only way."

And so it was that Freydis had all the men who came with Helgi and Finnbogi killed. Then she had the women brought out of the house.

"Give me that axe," said Freydis to one of her men. He gave it to her, and she killed each of the five women who had come with Helgi and Finnbogi.

Then Freydis, Thorvard, and their men went back to Leif's houses. When they arrived, Freydis said, "When we get back to Greenland, none of you are to breathe a word of what just happened. If you do, I will find you, and I will kill you. We will tell everyone that the others decided to settle here and that they gave us their ship to take our cargo home."

In the spring, Freydis and her crew loaded both ships with the goods they had collected during their sojourn in Vinland. They sailed with fair winds all the way back to Eiriksfjord, where Thorfinn Karlsefni was preparing to depart for Norway. Everyone looked at the cargo Freydis brought back with her, and all agreed that this was the greatest amount of goods anyone had yet brought home from Vinland, and by far the most valuable.

Freydis went back to her farm after rewarding her crew very generously so that they would not talk about what had happened in Vinland. Then Freydis resumed working her farm and taking care of her livestock.

Now, there were some among Freydis's crew who were unable to keep silent about what she had done. Soon enough, word spread that Freydis had had Helgi and Finnbogi's crew murdered and that she had killed all the women herself. Eventually, Freydis's brother Leif heard the story, and he was horrified. He had three of Freydis's crew arrested, and he tortured them until they told the whole story. When he had heard everything, Leif said, "I am not the one to punish my sister for her cruel deeds. But I think that her children and her children's children will not fare well. That shall be recompense enough."

Leif's words came true. When Freydis and Thorvard had children, everyone treated them badly because they expected them to behave as their mother had. And when those children had children of their own, people treated them badly as well for the same reason.

Thus ends the Vinland Sagas.

# References

Boult, Katharine F. *Heroes of the Northlands: Their Stories Retold.* London: J. M. Dent & Co., 1903.

Chadwick, Nora. *Stories and Ballads of the Far Past.* Cambridge: Cambridge University Press, 1921.

Edwards, Paul, and Hermann Pálsson, ed. and trans. *Arrow-Odd: A Medieval Novel.* New York: New York University Press, 1970.

Gathorne-Hardy, Geoffrey Malcolm, trans. *The Norse Discoverers of America: The Wineland Sagas.* Oxford: Clarendon Press, 1921.

Jones, Gwyn. *The Norse Atlantic Saga.* New ed. Oxford: Oxford University Press, 1964.

Kolodny, Annette. *In Search of First Contact: The Vikings of Vinland, the People of Dawnland, and the Anglo-American Anxiety of Discovery.* Durham: Duke University Press, 2012.

Kunz, Keneva, trans. "The Vinland Sagas." In *The Sagas of Icelanders: A Selection*, pp. 626–76. New York: Viking Penguin, 2000.

Magnusson, Magnus, and Hermann Pálsson. *The Vinland Sagas: The Norse Discovery of America.* New York: New York University Press, 1966.

Munch, Peter Andreas. *Norse Mythology: Legends of Gods and Heroes*. Trans. Sigurd Bernhard Hustvedt. New York: The American-Scandinavian Foundation 1926.

Pringle, Heather. "Evidence of Viking Outpost found in Canada." *National Geographic News* (19 October 2012). <https://www.nationalgeographic.com/news/2012/10/121019-viking-outpost-second-new-canada-science-sutherland/#close> Accessed 25 May 2020.

Reeves, Arthur Middleton, North Ludlow Beamish, and Rasmus B. Anderson, trans. *Norroena: The History and Romance of Northern Europe*. Vol. 15, *Vinland Edition*. n. c.: n. p., T. H. Smart, 1906.

Simpson, Jaqueline, trans. *The Northmen Talk: A Choice of Tales from Iceland*. London: Phoenix House, 1965.

Tolkien, Christopher, trans. *Saga Heidriks Konungs ins Vitra/The Saga of King Heidrik the Wise*. London: Thomas Nelson and Sons, Ltd., 1960.

Tunstall, Peter, trans. *The Saga of Hervor & King Heidrik the Wise*. In *The Complete Fornaldarsögur Nederlanda: Legendary Sagas of the Northland in English Translation*. <http://www.germanicmythology.com/FORNALDARSAGAS/HervararSagaTunstall.html> Accessed 8 April 2020.

Waggoner, Ben, trans. *The Hrafnista Sagas*. New Haven: Troth Publications, 2012.

Wallace, Birgitta. "The Norse in Newfoundland: L'Anse aux Meadows and Vinland." *Newfoundland and Labrador Studies* 19/1. Retrieved from https://journals.lib.unb.ca/index.php/NFLDS/article/view/140.

Here's another book by Matt Clayton
that you might be interested in

www.ingramcontent.com/pod-product-compliance
Lightning Source LLC
Chambersburg PA
CBHW020109240426
43661CB00002B/94